AF347758

26

[illegible] Tupraj [illegible] Maruti Nana [illegible] Michael [illegible] Amar Aotar [illegible] Andhe B. Mehta [illegible]
[illegible] Aunty Anjali Srivastava Arpan Khatadia Mariella Bhaskar's Parents Kermann's Parents Divjot's [illegible]
[illegible]'s Parents Pramjal Sahibjeet Jasnoor Riya Dhruv Rishabh Megha Anita Aunty Matko Sonpreet Rajshind [illegible]
[illegible] Bua James Urlini Happy Aunty Baby Chachi Nicholas Muhammad Rohyl Clament Roy Kudrat Amrit Uncle [illegible]
[illegible]Alessandro Ben Jeevanjot Jamisyn Brandon Shiho Lisa Alina Nivedita Gunali Bhavya Ehte Dylan Andrew Lee [illegible]
[illegible] Shelly Megan Kalhan Isabel Solin Isabella Etna Sahar Mann Nikita Khush Michael Saran Sukhman Thomas [illegible]
[illegible]anki Ma'am Sarah Tasha Sehaj Kate Johnson Mannat Dhaliwal Mannat Lumba Jasleen Singh Soeui Oh Shriya [illegible]
[illegible] Inderjeet Ma'am Inder Vaishaly Ma'am Ojaswini Kasam Chau Pham Savar Diksha Vishesh Poom Harjodh [illegible]
[illegible] Steven Chu Isabel Sakshi Agarwal Vaishakh Michael Barrese Lohit Satbir Ralph Jannan Kazmi Flin Judd [illegible]
[illegible]an Ibrat Tj Gagan Mannat Chaitanya Devika Chehek Manik Archit Aizad Amanat Tarun Tushar Duneep [illegible]
[illegible]eitrich Florian Dietrich Sukhman Tom Huntingford Jack M Zhang Inez David Liu Peeyush Dale Kabir [illegible]
[illegible] Michelle Andre Guy From Number 1 Steven Andre Jack Sutter Jim Cowie Harinder Ma'am Raymon [illegible]
[illegible] Suman Kelly Ashneet Nikhil Vineetha Gureet Pranav Je Jeremybalkaran Sarel Deepinder Guneet [illegible]
[illegible]bbar Maama Jessica Melvin Kim Bhaktawar Mahima Vibhu Sanjam Prabhnoor Chahal Khushi Chadha [illegible]
[illegible]egan Navneet Hugh Hugh Foster Molly Grace Tim Rodens Himank Harshita Shaurya Sambhav Tracy [illegible]
[illegible]annat Rishinandini Ananya Yashangi Sonu Maamu Monu Maamu Rajiya Maami Prajwal Rahul Diya [illegible]
[illegible]eru Latika Naman Minku Chachu Raman Chachi Sazia Sarah Jimmy Bua Navneet Chachi Beeba Ravjot [illegible]
[illegible] Jagjot Liz Annake Mark Irving Heather Philip Goad Roger Beeston Stuart King Adriana Shaira Afrida [illegible]
[illegible]souza Elias John Rigas Divar David Lavbourn Ryan Browne Anmol Ishrat Anushka Lena Sonam Dan [illegible]
[illegible]Tja Abhay Kennen Puma Yuvraj Saahil Jack Liam Abhimanyu Cameron Vaidehi Will Scobie Uda[illegible]
[illegible] Aikam Heaven Anmol Amana Mehek Jade Manmit Bhakti Aunty Aeshna Kritika Reetinder Parikshit [illegible]
[illegible]ikramraj Rishi Uncle Vicky Uncle Arjun Simran Raymon Gurpratap Shinkle Gurpriya Daanish Bindra Olivia [illegible]
[illegible]avinder Ma'am Kooner Sir Sartaj Prabhjot Dhananjay Sukhsagar Manjeev Maam Manjeet Maam Pahwa [illegible]
[illegible] Pa'am Shubhdeep Harsamar Vidhur Ishit Jayaprabha Ma'am Simarjeet Richa Ma'am Vidhiyotma Ravi [illegible]
[illegible]haiana Ma'am Nirbhav Sahiba Munish Nishant Gurshan Nitika Ma'am Prerna Ma'am Raiwinder Ma'am [illegible]
[illegible] Satpal Agam Gurmeher Gurfateh Abhimanyu Mann Mann Sir Upnit Kanika Maa Papa Jasleen Bhaskar Sidd[illegible]
[illegible] Daadu Chandan Bua Jyoti Bua Rajni Bua Naanu Naani Shintu Maamu Mintu Maamu Neeru Maami Hriday [illegible]
[illegible]shleen Pushpleen Manpreet Ranjit Fufa Gurleen Yuvraj Titu Fufa Jaskaran Balkirat Jasmeet Guntaniya [illegible]
[illegible]haran Mohini Eleanor Oscar Divjot Sheena Aunty Abir Abeer Simran Pandal Dolly Ma'am Kermann Aashna [illegible]
[illegible] Daanish Binayreet Vinaydeep Amran Tasavur Simrat Sohan Rebecca Krishma Rahat Amelia Chris Charley [illegible]
[illegible] David Calf Melissa Tan Carmen Duong Mj Simran Bec Baani Lydia Jarel Amanda Paul Katz Michelle [illegible]
[illegible]ouglas Giovanna Connor Yugam Karanbir Vikram Meher Bahl Vishwam Jaireet Gurkanwar Eunju Kim [illegible]
[illegible]tal Mrs Oh Sanya Anjali Ma'am Rajdeep Ma'am Sukirat Sir Harprabhjot Sir Niripjit Sir Jaqjit Sir [illegible]
[illegible] Nico Maha Taha Gursaya Sakshi Nanki Nehmet Lovneet Rohan Harshak Apurva Kester Nivar Kathe[illegible]
[illegible] Alba Johnson Carmel Abdullah Liam Grace Lily Evey Hamish Lynn Numair Ekam William Endrick [illegible]
[illegible]Maggie Georgia Hamzah Aishpreet Prabhjot Bhabhi Harseerat Bhabhi Ginny Gursahib Anhad Ashleigh [illegible]
[illegible]orge Riley Yui Sam Emilio Elijah Mihi Dan Crawford Heidi Sobhneek Nivan Aashween Andrew Pooja [illegible]
[illegible]anshika Prabekam Vanshika Raghumit Raghuraj Radhika Sanjeevan Anumit Noel Koula Jennifer Alex [illegible]
[illegible]oobaani Harkrit Harleen Ravneet Sophia Sarah Serine Sarah Inayat Sonu Chachu Rosy Chachi Raman [illegible]
[illegible]rev Prabhangad Saima Samnit Puneeta Ma'am Aaliya Coen Nakul Sangeeta Ma'am Rashmi Ma'am Anita Ma'am [illegible]
[illegible]preet Aunty Raju Bhayia Suraj Bhayia Baaj Manjeet Rai Ma'am Gursobha Young Ananya Khujneri [illegible]
[illegible]anir Samar Chachu Amit Sir Simran Ishita Xianke Bholi Aunty Grace Jasveen Ma'am Grant [illegible]
[illegible]Thom Krynen Kunal Suryajit Sangeeta Khanna Anchit Savu Bhaji Harnoor Gunjan Binny Bhaaji Oshin [illegible]
[illegible]rbana Gurkanwal Ma'am Rajinder Pal Devgon Sir Janyanjit Ray Zubin Mehta Harish Dhillon Japtej Seema [illegible]
[illegible]Pal Chiman Uncle Sumitra Aunty Abhaas Aastha Saurabh Anand Saurabh Aarya Mandy Mehboob Kabir [illegible]
[illegible]tice Rana Ma'am Rizwal Briener Mishween Aman Buttar Josh Budgen Bhanu Di Mehta Di Seema Sood Ma'am [illegible]

[illegible]ivastava Arpan Khatadia Mariella Bhaskar's Parents Kermann's Parents Divjot's Parents Siddh[illegible]
[illegible] Sahibjeet Jasnoor Riya Dhruv Rishabh Megha Anita Aunty Matko Sonpreet Raishind Aman Aunty [illegible]
[illegible]appy Aunty Baby Chachi Nicholas Muhammad Rohyl Clement Roy Kudrat Amrit Uncle Bronwyn Stocks [illegible]
[illegible] Jamisyn Brandon Shiho Lisa Alina Nivedita Gunali Bhavya Ehte Dylan Andrew Lee Anshal Khawar [illegible]
[illegible]abel Solin Isabella Etna Sahar Mann Nikita Khush Michael Saran Sukhman Thomas Martinello Ankit [illegible]
[illegible]sha Sehaj Kate Johnson Mannat Dhaliwal Mannat Lumba Jasleen Singh Soeui Oh Shriya Neelam Alex [illegible]
[illegible]der Vaishaly Ma'am Ojaswini Kasam Chau Pham Savar Diksha Vishesh Poom Harjodh Syrah Sajnee[illegible]
[illegible]akshi Agarwal Vaishakh Michael Barrese Lohit Satbir Ralph Jannan Kazmi Flin Judd Gianni Lyan[illegible]
[illegible]annat Chaitanya Devika Chehek Manik Archit Aizad Amanat Tarun Tushar Duneep Neelu Ma'am Cl[illegible]
[illegible]ietrich Sukhman Tom Huntingford Jack M Zhang Inez David Liu Peeyush Dale Kabir Parmar Butt[illegible]
[illegible] Andre Guy From Number 1 Steven Andre Jack Sutter Jim Cowie Harinder Ma'am Raymon Harleen Ma am [illegible]
[illegible]ly Ashneet Nikhil Vineetha Gureet Pranav Je Jeremybalkaran Sarel Deepinder Guneet Babbar Binny [illegible]
[illegible]essica Melvin Kim Bhaktawar Mahima Vibhu Sanjam Prabhnoor Chahal Khushi Chadha Navya Sapra [illegible]
[illegible]eman Hugh Foster Molly Grace Tim Rodens Himank Harshita Shaurya Sambhav Tracy Bhoomi Vasudev Mehta [illegible]
[illegible]inani Ananya Yashangi Sonu Maamu Monu Maamu Rajiya Maami Prajwal Rahul Diya Rajdeep Amitoze [illegible]
[illegible]aman Minku Chachu Raman Chachi Sazia Sarah Jimmy Bua Navneet Chachi Beeba Ravjot Johnny Chachu [illegible]
[illegible] Annake Mark Irving Heather Philip Goad Roger Beeston Stuart King Adriana Shaira Afrida Tom Meeha[illegible]
[illegible]Elias John Rigas Divar David Lavbourn Ryan Browne Anmol Ishrat Anushka Lena Sonam Dan Dasha [illegible]
[illegible]av Kennen Puma Yuvraj Saahil Jack Liam Abhimanyu Cameron Vaidehi Will Scobie Udav Naufal [illegible]
[illegible]eaven Anmol Amana Mehek Jade Manmit Bhakti Aunty Aeshna Kritika Reetinder Parikshit Hardaman [illegible]
[illegible] Rishi Uncle Vicky Uncle Arjun Simran Raymon Gurpratap Shinkle Gurpriya Daanish Bindra Olivia [illegible]
[illegible]arvinder Ma'am Kooner Sir Sartaj Prabhjot Dhananjay Sukhsagar Manjeev Maam Manjeet Maam Pahwa [illegible]
[illegible]aiana Ma'am Nirbhav Sahiba Munish Nishant Gurshan Nitika Ma'am Prerna Ma'am Raiwinder Ma'am [illegible]
[illegible] Satpal Agam Gurmeher Gurfateh Abhimanyu Mann Mann Sir Upnit Kanika Maa Papa Jasleen Bhaskar Sidd[illegible]
[illegible]di Daadu Chandan Bua Jyoti Bua Rajni Bua Naanu Naani Shintu Maamu Mintu Maamu Neeru Maami Hriday [illegible]
[illegible]hleen Pushpleen Manpreet Ranjit Fufa Gurleen Yuvraj Titu Fufa Jaskaran Balkirat Jasmeet Guntaniya [illegible]
[illegible]haran Mohini Eleanor Oscar Divjot Sheena Aunty Abir Abeer Simran Pandal Dolly Ma'am Kermann Aashna [illegible]
[illegible] Daanish Binayreet Vinaydeep Amran Tasavur Simrat Sohan Rebecca Krishma Rahat Amelia Chris Charley [illegible]
[illegible]adu David Calf Melissa Tan Carmen Duong Mj Simran Bec Baani Lydia Jarel Amanda Paul Katz Michelle [illegible]
[illegible]ouglas Giovanna Connor Yugam Karanbir Vikram Meher Bahl Vishwam Jaireet Gurkanwar Eunju Kim [illegible]
[illegible]tal Mrs Oh Sanya Anjali Ma'am Rajdeep Ma'am Sukirat Sir Harprabhjot Sir Niripjit Sir Jaqjit Sir [illegible]
[illegible] Nico Maha Taha Gursaya Sakshi Nanki Nehmet Lovneet Rohan Harshak Apurva Kester Nivar Kathe[illegible]
[illegible] Alba Johnson Carmel Abdullah Liam Grace Lily Evey Hamish Lynn Numair Ekam William Endrick [illegible]
[illegible]Maggie Georgia Hamzah Aishpreet Prabhjot Bhabhi Harseerat Bhabhi Ginny Gursahib Anhad Ashleigh [illegible]
[illegible]orge Riley Yui Sam Emilio Elijah Mihi Dan Crawford Heidi Sobhneek Nivan Aashween Andrew Pooja [illegible]

26

A collection of Poems and other Writings

Mannik Singh

To,

My Garden

Contents

Foreword

Dear Reader,

How does one truly understand oneself? Is it through writing, reflecting, introspecting, and contemplating life's conversations and events? To reopen closed chapters to dissect why you are the way you are? Can you only truly move forward by acknowledging the past and looking backwards? Within these pages, I am making an attempt.

I offer to you, contained within these pages, the echoes of the moments of past, the letters that never made it to the post, diary entries that I transformed into verses, the depths of my soul stripped bare. I offer to you moments of agony, adoration, and wistfulness, alongside confessions of my wrongdoings and my deepest insecurities.

Like the cover of this book, I am adorned with the memories of people, stories, and fleeting moments. Denying the influence of others on who I've become would be unwise. In my narratives, I become the echoes of others' perceptions— a dutiful son, a trustworthy brother, a loving yet insecure boyfriend, a reliable friend, a rebel grandchild, a detached cousin, a narcissistic douchebag, and a spectral memory, almost there but not quite. Yet, I am also what I wish for you to perceive. In the act of sharing ourselves we inevitably craft a multifaceted yet imperfect reflection of ourselves. There are facets of me I try to embrace and others I attempt to conceal, yet they're transparent to those who look closely.

This project is rooted in years of putting my thoughts onto paper. It has been a therapeutic practice that has helped me navigate the various chapters of my life. With the encouragement of friends, I've curated the snapshots of my life into this project, whimsically named "26".

Consider this foreword an invitation. Make yourself comfortable with a cup of tea or coffee. Pick up this book or set it down as often as you wish. The show is about to begin. Within, you may discover reflections of yourself interwoven with my personal journey—people known and those imagined. Throughout the pages of my book, you will encounter pixelated versions and tales of my life, whims, fantasies, and the mosaic of thoughts that I carry. Each poem is a puzzle piece, and I hope they come together like autumn leaves.

Prologue

Ladies, gentlemen & my non-binary pals
Please gather 'round as the show unveils.
I'm about to embark on a bit of a show and tell,
With tales that haunt me, making sleep a hard sell.

Open your eyes, look up at the sky.
Soaring on the rainbows, reaching the golden highs.
In search of the green-hatted man I roam,
Thrust into the rabbit hole, uncertain and alone.

I land atop magical toadstools, oh so grand!
They let out a deep sigh, as if they understand.
Pixie dust and spores up in the air,
Oh, What a magical sight, beyond compare!

Alice and Mad Hatter and garden tea soirées
Cheshire Cat smiles, and whispers of dismay.
Red and blue teacups alongside white sugar crystals.
Long days and nights, only time to frivol.

Dancing princesses in dresses of emerald hue.
Gatsbian dreams and Parisian sunsets too.
Winters in New York and Indian summer's rest,
Tales of love, heartbreaks, betrayals and fest.

Melbournian skies and golden dinner affairs.
Dandies and Quaintrelles, elegance that ensnares.
Familial complexities and tragic Achillean romances.
Curses spanning distances, longing for fresh warm chances.

Midnight strikes, fair-weathered friends fade,
Stolen toys and childhood shares, memories bade.
No finger-pointing, no blame to condemn,
Amongst myself and them, forgiveness must begin.

Ladies, gentlemen & my non-binary pals,
The stories I share are of feelings deep and mal.
I pray upon totem trees, clutch monkey paws,
Pining for solace amidst all my fatal flaws.

IV

About the Narrator

The Great Gatsby, like Gatsby's glory, overrated and missed
like misplaced affections,
Books, a fickle affair, akin to his quest for his muse.
A bit of a bitch, this Daisy character, let's be real,
or so the story goes, or so it is told.

Nick, the storyteller, the observer, Intriguing, isn't he?
A mirror, perhaps?
Pity money he and I, both, seem to collect effortlessly.
That's the pitfall of being a narrator.
"What happened, where, and when?"
Memories, or fragments of illusion?
Was it sunny, or clouds shrouding the sky? The clarity of
memory can be a foggy terrain, or is it a deliberate fog?
Confusion lingers, and the narrator pirouettes on.

Moments, captured, then blurred by time's embrace.
How much of me must be cloaked for comprehension?
Do I seek sympathy, or play into the drama I'm accused of?
How much truth to unveil, how much to cloak?
Layers upon layers, like a Russian doll of perception.

My therapist, sister, and friends chorus in unison - "Stop
playing the victim!"
I'm urged to cease manifesting sadness, my sister's griping
that my penchant for writing melancholy breeds a self-fulfilling
prophecy.
Yet, if happiness were my muse, would joyous prose flow
effortlessly?
It seems, happiness wears a monotonous mask; sadness, a palette
of hues to craft tales both haunting and beautiful.

Anyway, as a bit of a critic of books, each a gamble in the
literary maze. Gatsby missed, just like he missed Daisy,
But maybe, in truth, the miss was the other way 'round.

Buttermilk.

A Fort

Mannik Singh| 26 | Buttermilk

Today, my sister and I built a fort.
We imagined it stood on the edge of the water on a port.
We filled it with toys, dolls and pillows.
Mumma fed us fryums by the kilo.
Under the fairy lights, we slept, our dreams very short.

My Garden

My garden is full of flowers I tend to.
Marigold fields, tulip and petunia patches.
Terracotta tiles line the bed where dreams are sown,
A sanctuary - where nature and my soul catches.

In my garden, I revel and I cry with zest.
Lush patches of green grass, with early morning dew.
Under the hibiscus tree, I sit on a bamboo chair with my
favourite tea,
playing scrabble, writing poetry and learning about lives old
and new

In my garden, daisy bushes spring bright,
I pluck a handful and display them with all my might.
Not once letting me down with their fragrance so nice -
the white lilies in the middle, talking to them, always such a
beautiful delight.

Poppies and memories of sprinkler splashes.
The dahlias, The sunflowers and the crimson-coloured roses in a
riot.
Sweet magnolias, familiar in the soft twilight.
A canvas of hues, making my garden a vibrant quiet.

In my garden, I spend my summer evenings with sweet lemonade.
My majestic olive tree whispers, mend the fence with care
Along the side of my room - A bougainvillea vine climbs
Each morning, the sun rays cast an enchanting magenta stare.

In my garden, a remedy blooms for every ailment's plight,
lavender by my bed, under moonlight's gleam,
rajnigandha whispers, jasmine at night holds sway.
A jolly vibe, a tranquil dream.

Tending to these flowers, as they tend to me
With care, with love, embracing serenity

In my garden, wilted and dry plants, not discarded with
disdain.
Roots stay grounded, with hope to bloom again.
Gathering bulbs, ready for a better spring,
Love awaits when the time is right to begin.

Shiny Toy, Soft Toy

My Shiny Toy, Soft Toy,
in a pristine package — untouched and unmarked.
My Shiny Toy, Soft Toy,
irresponsibly snatched away before I could explore.
My Shiny Toy, Soft Toy,
in front of me, they held and broke its bones.
My Shiny Toy, Soft Toy,
Insane! They are killers of joy.
My Shiny Toy, Soft Toy,
I will seek your vengeance.
My Shiny Toy, Soft Toy,
I lie awake in the night, planning a vigilante's revenge.
My Shiny Toy, Soft Toy,
in the twilight, knives I will deploy.
My Shiny Toy, Soft Toy,
I will avenge your plight.

Questions

I don't understand how you were never annoyed,
by my constant questions, repeated every car ride -
to the market, to the farm, to the hills every summer.

How do rainbows form, so pretty and bright?
Why does rain fall from the sky?
How are babies made, do you know?
Honey lasting, how does it go?

Why am I here, how did I start?
Sunlight's warmth, what's in its heart?
Why did the balloons bring me fear?
Why does the light make me cheer?

Thank you for being patient with me, and for
taking me on rides
to the gardens, to the fare, to the new towns every winter.

Praying

Evening prayers, incandescent lamps;
Photos on the glass shelf.
Sweet orange balls, *Gurbaani* flows,
Amritsar's essence in my ears it bestows.
Incense swirls, dhoop's graceful rise,
Clouds in the ceiling's pristine ties.
Holy water droplets on upholstery rest,
Some glistening on the white marble beneath my step.
Another Tuesday, another week –
Where I was praying,
like my grandmother.
She held this ritual close to her,
would read sweet *Baanis* from the sacred *Granth*;
and pray for the family's prosperous future.
I sat alone, in solitude.
Closed doors, in the only place I found –
some piece of silence in this chaos –
My sanctuary, my restroom.
I prayed for something different.
I promised things I'd sacrifice for if they'd come true.
Whispers of "never again," a solemn vow,
hoping the *paramatama* hears me now.

Kick

Mannik Singh| 26 | Buttermilk

You are no God!
You cheat and lie, you break and whine.
You did not deserve to have your feet touched.
But you forced -
Imposed them against her temple.
You're a *Rakshasa*.

Jasnik

Born on the 8th 'neath May's sweltering skies,
to an iron-willed mother, in a town of mystical tales.
A cherished gift, foreseen in his sister's vision true,
Cradled by his golden fields, he was their heir, after all,
His father's rage wielding a bat in the *Laal Kothi*'s shadow,
where he resided, inheriting his grandfather's demeanour at his
core.

A tender soul whisked away to a city afar, yet fear dared not
settle in his core.
I heard his happiest times were under different hued skies,
Yet, love drew him back under the *kothi*'s red shadow.
His sparkling eyes recount his wildest myths and tales.
His bullying made a few cry, "Jerk," exclaimed by them all!
Boarding school pranks, unsolicited, crass; he admits they're
true.

Anecdotes spun like silken threads, weaving tales of opulence
and folly; true -
of a life lived — spoiled and bratty, fruits peeled, cut, and
cored—
served on a silver platter. In turn, the sisters got a return
on all
their love - drenched farewell outfits, torn book pages,
protection from wandering eyes under the Punjabi skies.
As the lore goes - none dare touch him, lest they live to tell
the tale.
Naturally, the man of the house protected them from any grey
shadows.

In middle-school, his father's collapse anchored him to the
Laal Kothi. A shadow
on the youngest of four! Life's trials testing his true
self. I felt the weight of his brow damp with sweat, after
hearing the tales
of a boy in turbans in shades of red, being cored
of his innocence - clouding his childhood skies,
swiftly turning him into a man, chasing life's daily bread for
all.

Yet, the child within endured, resilient in the face of tumult,
after all.
In the wee hours of the morning, bets had cast their sullen
long shadow.
His mother's bat a harsh teacher under the tangerine skies,
When I hear unheroic stories, I presume what they hold is
somewhat true.
Ten rupees wagered by him and his friends, blank exams, defiance
at their core,
He bore his mother's gashes smiling as recounted are the tales

Continuing on the dappled yellow brick road, unfurling his
metamorphic tales,
His mother, to make him an honest man, decided to wed him to a
beautiful woman in front of all -
to impart invaluable lessons, nurturing his heart and core.
Beneath the February sun, he shed his solitary shadow.
What they say about marriages perhaps holds true,
She emerged as solace; brought with her ambrosial buttermilk
skies.

And, when I arrived, for me, he wished for brighter tales,
where light takes over the shadows.
To embrace all of life, void of fear, eternally content and
true;
To have a resilient core, always connected, chance to paint my
skies my favourite shades of yellow.

My Faith

Kindness, beauty, love, and my concept of God are present in
everything—
the water, the land, the air we breathe,
the person you love, the person across the street,
the animal the car inadvertently struck dead,
the animal lying beside you as you sleep,
the rocks, the plants, the fish,
the person who birthed you, the person who killed,
the person in the polaroid frozen in time, locked in a kiss on
your cheeks,
the person you went on a solitary date with before finding your
current companion,
the person who stood you up waiting at the restaurant -
The person who caused you to stumble, the one who cheated,
the girl you ran into on the first day of university,
the guy you graduated alongside.
The cosmos, your friends, your sister,
the reflection in the mirror, and the mirror itself.

So, all I do is respect and treat everybody as I've been
taught.
I close my eyes and utter the Name and do *Seva*.

Son Pari

Mannik Singh| 26 | Buttermilk

Yellow, glorious, Golden!
Winged sparkly fairy –
in my secret garden!
Come save me, when I rub the crystal,
hold my hand as we fly across the ocean.
Sparkles glisten and the air feels divine!
When you whisk me to a different place –
away from the Haunted Palace each night.
With a swish of a wand, and fairy dust so nice
The diamonds dim in comparison to the shine you beguile.
Your magic is sweet, it makes me feel so safe –
despite Cruella's tricks, that stirs panic within.
The evil witch schemes with plans I can't fathom,
But I sleep assured, knowing you and Aaltu are near
Keeping black magic away from here.

Edgar Allen Poe – The Haunted Palace

Summer of 2000 something

In the quiet night, weariness descends,
sweat traces paths on a tired face's bends.

Beneath the moon, transformers groan,
Overheated whispers in the dark are known.

Under the weight of a dead battery's plight,
The generator sighs in the still of the night.

Newspaper fans the fading embers,
In the haze of drowsiness, time remembers.

Marble's cool touch, a comforting embrace,
She stirs in 3 hours, with a dawn to chase.

Amidst the mosquitoes' songs, down to the car we stray,
AC hums gently, guiding sleep our way.

Dawn on the 11th

April night arrived, carrying the weight of anxious morn,
A choice to make, between leaving or being buried forlorn.
Do I regret that night, or the dawning light?
Not a single ounce of remorse for my hasty flight.

An act of defiance, to prove I'm no wretched con,
Not here to pilfer the fortunes they've selfishly drawn.
No regrets for tears shed, no remorse for my role,
Yearning to soar like a dove, seeking peace as my goal.

Months had passed, dreaming of escape from it all,
Where bullets attacked the woman who'd shield me from the
brawl.
Chasing shattered fragments of summer dreams,
Money and royalty hold no sway, as it seems.

That April night, I slept upright in restless slumber,
Arms clutching weapons, packing bags with socks that murmur.
No regrets for the tears they shed, perhaps they deserved more,
For overlooking mine, my whole life, at their core.

The ensuing morn was a scorpion's den, a haze of blue,
Yellow lights, marble stairs, a new upholstered view.
Stray dogs barked, mine wept upon my lap,
Not the ending I envisioned, a different kind of trap.

Yet change was born, both within and around,
Running wasn't my desire, but defiance profound.
The dawn of the eleventh, a feverish dream,
One I don't regret, no matter how it may seem.

I wanted them to regret what they did, to a boy of fifteen
years,
And to his younger sister, bearing the weight of taunting
jeers.
I loved them less, his sisters made their claim,
While his mother uttered words, "solely driven by cash's aim".

Insults hurled and gashes thrown, by kin, oh so unkind,
Hence, before the dawn of 11th, I chose to leave behind.
I decided to relinquish my name, to heed their voice.
I became what they moulded, what they bestowed,
But only that, I vowed, their narratives to unload.

When we were younger

We don't hold certainty's key,
Yet whispers speak, as I've heard,
Of an ancient line of witches, etched in my family's history,
Weaving magic, visions stirred.
In slumber's realm, they would behold
the living, ethereal hosts conversed,
gifting voices to ghostly apparitions - bold.
Sorcery passed down, blessed and cursed.

Within our veins, those powers reside.
In youth's embrace, we felt their might,
When amaltas blooms bloomed, golden and wide,
-My sister and I-
As petals unfurled, in fragrant air,
My sister sensed unions blossoming, sweet and rare,
Like birds and bees, her intuition aware,
A scent of promise, love's tender affair.

But fate's rustle found solace with me,
The fall, the doom, in shadows revealed,
A harbinger of endings -
Where yellows withered, their life congealed.
As relationships waned, I foresaw the decay,
In seasons' turn, a sorrowful play,
Where beauty's vibrance faded away,
And nature's cycle embraced the grey.

Trophy Child

Get that trophy, child.
You are our trophy
child, get those medals,
We'll display them on our mantle.
Golden or silver or bronze
It's fine! The reflections and glimmer
Enough to flicker pride
in our eyes, wow us with your dazzling sight.
You are our trophy
child, button up your shirt, dance and sing;
write poetry, excel at science.
Be a doctor, an architect, a lawyer,
whatever you like, we don't mind.
Don't swerve off the path,
We'll fence it if you'd like.
Keep cycling on the blue road,
and keep your eyes straight and narrow,
Do you need blinkers or something more?
You are our trophy
child, would you like to juggle for us?
How about you stand on the tightrope,
and play guitar for us?
We have heard you're malleable –
would you perhaps perform trapeze for us?
You are our trophy
child, find us one more trophy child.
Be with them and climb that tree
build a house and that berth for those sheets,
Whatever frame or colour you like –
give us more trophy
childs. You are our trophy
child, don't let us down, don't you sigh.

Hands

If you wanted my hands,
you should have chopped them off.
My soul, untarnished, didn't merit such
touches, masked deceit, while I feigned a slumber's touch.
Not in dreams, but awake, aware,
Beneath the roof of supposed care.
Tainted essence, innocence betrayed,
In your hands, trust decayed.
Should have severed them off, if it's all you craved -
You should've realised the value of righteousness,
you weren't even that tall or mighty wise,
You should've left me be - asleep, unshaken
unaware , un-paralysed. I was also just a boy. My soul
didn't deserve what you'd put me through.

I sit to write a eulogy

It is all in my head, a flicker of what could have been.
An untimely death of a would have been, it's a proper sin.
I would have loved you, held you for a lifetime.
I need to blame someone for this heinous crime.

The painted colours of the warm kitchen are now down the sink.
The smell of rose & dahlia petals now makes me sick.
The starry white bed sheets, now tainted yellow.
I hate rolling down clover-covered Monticello.

I would have written you a novella, and a thousand stories so
sweet,
I would have showered you with chocolate-covered candy treats.
I would have taken you on walks around the world.
Each night on our living room sofa we would have curled.

"Your smile shone the brightest," everyone said.
Your golden glue held together every broken bit, it was the
love that you freely spread.
Your bright eyes now lack the sparkle.
Seeing your lifeless body makes me startled.

I sit to write a eulogy, a beautiful ode so sweet
My precious love,
It has taken me a while,
I have mulled over the style
Do I paint or shall I sit to write?
How do I capture it? It has to be right –
but nothing will be.

Identity Erasure

Past life chases, forced name change, erasure of identity.
All the mementos of maiden life, left behind, at home to never
Return, never sought, bound by ties, married to customs.
Another bruise, another scar, happily received,
Marital bliss, bless my soul and hers and his, oh the irony.
Jest, jokes, a mockery of familial bouquet of trust and
familiarity.
Everything, all at once, had to be present, to be bequeathed.
Entwined lives, forceful changing values, changing faces, a
charade to be accepted into
Traditions, society's acceptance, another thing she had to
relinquish.

Scrub

In my hometown,
Once, many moons ago,
I believed I oozed the hue –
the muddy brown of my fields,
from which I had just emerged.

So, I scrubbed more vigorously,
aiming to wash myself
of the colours embedded in my skin —
Pumice Stone, Loofah, nails delving beneath.

I recognised early on
That worldly success often favoured whiteness,
Whiteness promised love, liberty;
unlocking gates to the world's embrace.
My brown skin, a potential source of trouble.

Back then, it wasn't solely about that,
It was about the subtle remarks,
Advising us kids to shun the sun,
Deeming dark skin as poverty's badge,
While lighter shades crowned with majesty.

These notions infiltrated through media,
Via TV adverts, storybooks,
And Grandma's tales—
A tale of a dark crow, submerging in the pool of Amritsar,
Emerging transformed into a white swan.

Thus, in my hometown,
Once, many moons ago,
When I thought I exuded the tint
of the muddy brown of my fields,
that I had just come from

I seized the moment and scrubbed more vigorously,
Aiming to purge myself
of the colours embedded in my skin—
Pumice Stone, Loofah, nails delving beneath.

Knucklehead

Knucklehead, killjoy, carcinogenic catastrophe.
A misery-toned filmstrip playing in the theatre of my childhood
reality.
Repugnant, ruthless gashes on my face, inflicted by you, deeply
scarred.
Absurdity of the highest kind! A fraternal bond forever marred.
Nightly, for a decade, I lay awake, seeking ways to forget this
incurable malady.

Jim-Jams

Jovially, her heart skips amidst blossoming daisy blooms fields,
Afternoon sweet lemonade. Relishing Jim-Jams and spiced milk
tea.
Singing, and dancing and tugging at my legs and my round
cheeks.
Lengthy conversations freeing us from the doll house mockery.
Entwined shoe laces, we tumble together towards the finish
line's liberation.
Enveloped by our cherished blankets, losing ourselves in
nutcracker's castle.
Nightly, I stand, guarding your door, protecting you and your
lovely dreams.

I was too scared of you
To love you.

Only Them

In their presence, my mind clouds up with
sudden darkness - a volatile *haneri*,
it thunders and it rumbles
rain comes crashing on the tepid ground.
And it cools, and dissipates as quickly as it came
leaving only the distraught soil behind.
How can they extract empathy from within me?

An itch in my ears whispers offering them a knife,
and to place my wrist before them; surrender.
My shoulder strains from the strings they hold.
They built me up, what an excuse to chisel me down.
How do I reconcile compassion with contempt?

The strings turn into invisible *zanjeers*, that
wrap around me, tied to reinforced concrete.
I struggle to roar amid the weight around my neck-
leaving me mute. Sometimes, the night sky gestures
that I should escape, pick the lock and run away!
An eternal departure. Isn't it tempting -
to fade away; to never reappear?

And then I look in the mirror and see their eyes,
torn up and in tears -
Perhaps an easy exit lies in the embrace of death,
Yet, that would sow seeds of agony on both fronts,
Leaving a trail of sorrow that nothing will erase.
Where does one start to mend a doomed connection?

Home 1.2

And on Sundays, in November, when it is only
beginning to get chilly in *Chandi*, I crave the tepid droplets
of mustard oil dripping in my hair
being massaged into my scalp – with nimble fingers,
like dancers in flight, my mother's hands weaving tales
in my ears and my head of
lives lived, being lived and to be lived.
My muscles sigh in sweet relief –
troubles retreat, unraveling the knots in my mind, releasing
hush –
whispering care in my ears as the warm oil
trickles down the side of my head.

I crave it, like I crave Kulfi, the one on the sticks –
freshly taken out of an obelisk mould, on a random thursday
afternoon
in July – under scorching heat, when no life flutters outside
the window,
the siestian lull traverses through the AC's constant hum –
you might hear a faint ringing of Kulfi Vaala's cart
around 4 o' clock. You just have to be lucky.

And then It comes crawling to me, as I sit with chai in my
hands –
sifting through childhood memories, needing a moment to ponder
& pause
I want to weave a hammock out of
bougainvillea vines on which love grew in playgrounds
and I want to rest in the March spring – tie my hammock
on both sides to the tall white barked eucalypts –
and become a silhouette against the lake in the North.
I'll watch the middle aged uncles and aunties,
brisk walking, march-pasting, controlled breathing, not
saluting –
no drums that keep beating, my mind is at peace.

A Hand-me-down Person

Mannerisms,
Diction, curve of smile.
Words, threaded into sentences -
Enunciation,
rolling of tongue.
The mouth that dances between 'v' & 'w'.
Lisp, a gentle stutter.
Accents.
The way he utters "staff",
His forehead crinkles.
Sister's playful slangs,
Father's confident gait,
grandfather's stoic ways of sitting,
Mother's varied emotions,
grandma's unwavering faith.
Daadi Bua's spirited temper.
A hand-me-down Person.

Short-Bread.

Deodar Trees

Each year, the pine needles fell from the sky,
draping the mountain valley sides with a green quilt.
Amidst the crackling flames, laughter danced in the air –
coiling with stories and memories shared, it was a timeless
affair!
Surrounded by friends, an inseparable "we".
Under the moon-lit skies, our hearts felt free.

On our annual trip to the Himachal, the trees have seen me grow
into my own. They have witnessed the laughter and the love
blossom
and shown. Beneath the starry canopy, and the Deodars'
silhouette stage –
my friends and I have endured storms that raged, tears shed,
and coming of age.

The moss-covered barks, the drizzled pine cones have been my
constant
each Summer –
May & June. Deodar Trees, oh my allies sweet,
please carry our stories beyond our reach.
Soar them skyward, and take them beneath our feet.
Beyond our years, become our eternal carriers, ever profound.

Playground Grass

Kindred colours of childhood playground grass.
                         Captured and pulled -
Esoteric memories. Treasured, withered and eventually forgotten.
Relieve the pain, relive the happiness, revel on the swing-set
                         and touch the -
Moss-covered red walls, grey gabion rocks. fog enveloped Ashokas.
Always playing tricks, ring around the Rosies, chasing monkeys,
Nearly catching you, not quite as quick as your wit or your
                         playful skip.
Naughty charades. Hide and seek.

April 9th

On April 9th,
in the schoolyard,
my memories flutter and frolic,
like a jezebel waltzing outside music room
where we were sat in the shade.
You gracefully offered me a sandwich with sunshine
reflecting in your gaze.
It was simple kindness wrapped in moments of sweet affection,
In the music room's roar, a flicker of love's shy glimmer.
your eyes spoke louder than the school bell's toll,
In bumble bee uniforms, a cacophony of tiny kindergarten souls.
Regret lingers in the air, the choir of little bees goes by,
I wish I hadn't declined, oh, how time can make us sigh.
I don't think you recall that day, a chance so slim,
Yet, every April 9th, my memories swim
and I float like a jezebel, flitting my wings.

Sixteen Again

Sometimes, I find myself circling the same quad, as I did
10 years ago, I stood on the precipice,
Alone; I lingered, silent I fell
broken by the words of my nemeses.

Sometimes, in my dreams, I am sixteen again
standing against the rusty rails of the spiral stairs.
My thoughts and I hung in turbulence.
I could've leaped but lacked courage.

I walk round and round in a hamster wheel –
Abandoned by my peers, I thought,
and asked myself the question ever so –
Where did my merry go?

"Gay!"

For six years, you wielded "Gay!" as a weapon,
In classrooms filled with ignorance, where stabs were a daily
session.
A humanist trait turned into a derogatory knife,
But strangely, your words don't cut as deep in my life, anymore.

Its been a decade since! I hear the rumours stirring still and
some more,
Let's go back to school, shall we? I think it's time to settle
the score.
Let me educate you, I'm good at it, for your knowledge is frail,
More than a noun, my identity's stable, let me unveil.

Your attempts to revile fall flat,
My resilience is stronger than your petty spat.
It is basic knowledge and I'll break it further down
for a mind that is stuck in a juvenile town.

Sex, a term both verb and noun,
Organs at birth, and something you seem to have renounced.
Gay, when men adore men's charms,
Lesbian, when women lock more than just arms.

Bisexual, pansexual, breaking the norms,
Liking everyone, no care for gender forms.
Asexuality, a spectrum, again, of a genuine disinterest,
But your paltry understanding, it seems to persist.

Gender is an expression beyond anatomy's frame,
Cis, trans, intersex, not just a game.
Cis, comfortable in the skin you've known,
Trans, correcting mistakes to what it should've been from the
get-go.

Intersex is a blend of both worlds divine,
Yet your IQ, stuck at the age of nine.
Your insults, a mix of confusion and blunder,
Gender and sexuality, you wildly plunder.

Misunderstandings, I forgive once more,
For your bullying, I see is more ignorance for sure.
A doofus with less wit than a goldfish, you see
fly away you stupid bumblebee.

She is pretty, She seems soft,
She seems like the girl that would make me calm,
She'll fit right in, understand my kin,
She's a beauty in every attire,
Even if she chooses to not inspire.

She is smart, She is kind.
She makes me want to kiss her mind.
She smells so good, I love her eyes in a twirl,
She sings so sweet, knows each word's swirl.
In her handwriting, secrets unfold.

Damp Shoes

Burning fervour of youthful anger, unrestrained, only I behold
Heartrending moments, tears restrained, resilience I uphold.
Amidst ashy lungs, filled with smoke, I plead with you to cease
Stars shimmering around the campfire, laughter echoing beneath a
Kaleidoscope of shiny lights in the sky above,
Amidst mockery of the next morn, you cursed & I chuckled in
your face,
Rainfall in the night, soaking your camera and shoes on the
final evening.

RED

For months, they encircled me like vultures during recesses and
breaks,
Each day, they hurled red-hot words, acrid currant of gestures,
Hosing on me acid raindrops, burning and greying the picture
of my technicolour schoolyard.

They believed they could persist,
judging me harshly on the
way I walked, the way I talked, –
a raisin jest that left a bitter taste.

I didn't want to engage, hob-nobbing with guys of their class;
So I, an outcast, was stamped with two triangles on the back of
both my hands –
in shades of Red – Pink & Coquelicot,
my scarlet letter, I'd walk around with for everyone to know

and recognise and be paraded around. They tied me to the back
of
the bandwagon – my walk of shame, a tired blush,
on my mahogany skin –
rough, harsh, being chiselled, until I couldn't any more.

They relentlessly pushed me to the precipice, scalding my
spirit,
But their persistent carving only sharpened my resolve,
upon those cream stairs, beside the carmine building,
My fury eventually erupted with molten lava so fierce.

In a surge of rage, I struck the ringleader in his crimson
shirt,
A scarlet hue adorned his nose, his eyes mirrored my own,
Dragged to the principal's office, their bravado fading,
replaced by a silent waltz of regrets, my eyes sang fearless
truths,
The blood staining the cold concrete still bears witness to my
rebellion,
Echoes of my revolt linger on the rusty rails.

They're Coming!

Hide, hide!
Beneath the shroud of night's cloak,
For they approach, shadowed fiends on the prowl.
Who?
The specters, myriad and nameless.
The phantasms, the revenants, the shadows of past.

They advance, sinuous and silent,
like serpents sinning through the grass.
Like scorpions surfacing from their roost,
Stealthily, insidiously. crawling up the bedstead,
Cover your ears and nose!
They'll nest in your nasal sinuses.

They're imminent,
Like night terrors lurking in obscurity,
Clowns with balloons floating with bright red smiles in space –
Taking shelter in the recesses of your psyche,
The look-alike wanderers from your history.

They'll contort your sinews,
They will quicken the beat of your heart.
A leaden weight upon your brow,
As you will tremble in apprehension.

Your soul ensnared, it seeks escape,
but you can't find a way out,
the egress's eluded by dark hazy mist,
For how long can the blanket keep you safe?

A photograph

Photos, like fossilised scrolls frozen in time ,
Carrying the testimonies of crime beyond our lives,
Capturing moments, and the ones that linger outside.
I analyse the evidence, tracing curves of happy smiles.

A February night, scattered fairy lights,
glass jar candles held in hands, tight,
mementos of our last times.
A 1960s gym hall, blue walls; ceilings and all,

You donned a sari dipped in shades –
matching the ones concealed within my turban's folds.
A chance synchronicity, unspoken in months past.
Your boyfriend's disapproval hung between us.

It was funny, though, that he wore the colours that didn't
compliment you,
In fact, he didn't compliment you.
His gaze rarely found its way to you, lost in the sea of
mismatched shades,
it was a stark contrast to the way my eyes sought,
the nuances in your every movement.

In a frozen frame of that night's photograph,
We posed, smiles masking the fractures in our hearts.
Behind the façade of joy, your silent plea echoed,
A request to disentangle my hand from the curve of your waist,
A phantom limb, a spectre haunting the photo's edge,
Falling as the camera captured our fleeting moment.

The plastered smile on my face wanes,
questions of happiness emerge in my brain.
I inquire the applause for our class's celebration in my mind,
And fail to remember the music and the creaking floorboards from
that night.

Paper Trail

A whispered caution to erase your tracks –
Rip the sheets from the depths of your notebook,
Expunge the imprints, leave no trace,
Graphite whispers secrets – Shhh! A dangerous embrace.

Schemes and truths, once shown, got to hit the road.
Burn those pages, else they'll come to burn you.
If you can, don't even put pen to paper –
Purge every trace, leave no evidence to chance.
Wipe clean the ears that might eavesdrop keen,
For swift retribution, the shadows convene.

A diary in the hands of a bored girl, can be so devastating.

Our dog teleports!

My dog is one sensible creature,
she sits with mum and wipes her tears,
and then wags her tail and brings her cheer.
And when mum gives her treats, her face puckers neat!

She shines when chasing things she finds,
Spares no pillow, thong, or a piece of lime.
She plays with my sister and tugs on the leash –
so much so, she once dragged her across the street.

She is a psychic, knows how my grandma is feeling,
then tip-toes or jogs or bounces, paying her reverence,
sincere.
She takes after Dad, sleeping day and night,
Snoring loudly, waking neighbours and guests alike.

Around me, she jumps and circles maniacally,
Side-eyeing, judging all of my oddities.
Teaming up with friends, they bully me fine,
but I take my revenge when it's bath time!

Her puppy eyes flare as I scrub her clean,
Bolts towards us, shaking off water, and then she sprints
around the house rubbing against sofas to dry herself off.
Of course, mum gets angry, and she gets a proper scoff –

In sadness, I think, she leaves for hours,
Having us form a search party, looking for her in the dark.
She reappears from the forest with weeds, branches and friends
bizarre,
Oh, dear Lord, our little star!

Sometimes, when the doors are locked and she's chilling
outside,
Somehow, she winds up in my sister's walk-in, she mysteriously
climbed?
We jump in an instant at her sight, and damn do we scream,
"Our dog teleports, Holy Shit!"

Hypocrite

Call me a fag,
call him gay.
Judge his gait
laugh in my face.
Teach me to walk
I'll teach that slut - purity.

Put a ring on her finger
until "I do"s hehe.

Intervene, "Save Her"
slap her, savour
fifteen, righteous, clean.

Make me cry it's fantastic -
building character for my autobiography.

Judge him on his weight.
Judge myself, slap my face.
We hate -
we'd kill to fit.

~~Doctor~~ Architect

Weariness would descend down my forehead, nightly
my muscles started to spasm, holding the
stethoscope pressed against the door, the floor,
trying to gauge if there is still some pulse,
traversing through the cracks in the walls.

I wasn't a good doctor, because I couldn't heal –
couldn't stop the bleed, couldn't dress the wounds that
I thought were mine to fix.
Why wouldn't you believe? The scabs still ooze
with the clear yellow-y goo, I couldn't even hold my sight.

I tried multiple times, to make you reflect, with a compass
drawing lines on my skin. I told you I wasn't a good surgeon –
lacking precision
but the shapes on my arm were pretty pictures that I hoped to
one day use
to build the crackless walls around my soul –
double brick, unrendered – raw and red
like the colour of my skin, the proof.

I promise, I will design better walls, with windows
opening at my whim, lovely sashes, double hung,
Insulated internal walls unlike the ones I'd grown up in.
Brick boundary walls, with a daffodil yellow front door.
Timber screens, Persian rugs, Royal blue painted
verandah fence that's sufficiently tall.

Daffodils.

Summer afternoon lull, winter evening chill.
Green grass and dodging the sprinklers splashes.
Terracotta pots with peonies and sweetpeas.
Up three flights, dodging the artefacts of all kinds -
golf clubs, books, even his dog's droppings,
what a quirky plight!
Dappled shadows on the blue wall against the fading light.
On the balcony high, three friends behold,
Sunset hues unfold, as two puff, bold.
In a darkened room, red eyes seek predestination,
Existential talks weave through the haze with unwavering
dedication.

Manipulator

I spin.
I am a spinner in a sufi dance,
or an island dancer, surrendering himself
to the Gods for it to pour.
My fields lie dry, crops near demise,
My bell's tolling brings no relief,
Nor does devotion ease my cries;
I unleash my tears at my will,
twisting them like the rings around their finger,
the ones that they have to wear.
I have spun the tales, twisted words
from the holy books, singing in a hymnal chorus.
I whirl in my white garb, praying for the fog to appear,
envelope me and rise, and rise, and rise,
until it disappears and so do I.
I have been crafting opportunities with each turn,
making promises with Him
to rewrite the destiny at my whim.
The clouds appear, in shades of grey –
the sticks I rubbed ignite,
serving my will—
I spin, like a sufi dancer, so do my sticks
arms spread outwards, head up towards the night
I spin like a sufi dancer,
and keep changing the stars in my skies.

Pink

Seated cross-legged on crisp white sheets,
Upon red and blue dhurries,
I methodically check off an invisible list.
Must buy, must discard, must never see again,
tucked away in my closeted den.
My list gets punctuated by the final ardaas,
My mother's paath - a prelude to my departure -
Seeking blessings, inviting those that I have to say goodbye to
the neighbours, the relatives, all the uncles and aunties
from the neighbourhoods we've lived in
in this big small city,

Gup-shup, after langar,
"Be cautious," they caution, "in your connections,"
Added to my checklist: guard your birthdate,
Your financial standing, shield your emotions.
My mind swells with this newfound wisdom, a burgeoning egg,
Threatening to burst through my hot pink turban.

A neighbourhood aunty, an Australia return,
In tones both candid and earnest,
Forgets her list, yet speaks her truth:
"Steer clear of pink down under,
It's reserved for a certain ilk,
It marks you *thus*, as *this* or *that*,"
the baby, the fuschia, the watermelon, the coral,
they don't discriminate
in any shade, because you don't want
to be giggled at for being *that*.
        Because we giggle at people for being *that* (unsaid)

No, aunty, I'm set to unfurl
My hot pink turban, fling it wide,
To aid those scaling my glass tower.
I am planning a queer tea party aloft,
Plotting world domination, with a giggle.
hehe x

A Comfortable Nest

Sitting on a bench in the park;
I saw a tiny bird making a new nest –
with leaves and branches, gathering nature's debris
in swift moments, crafting a new home to be.
Right below a new eucalptus tree.

Did it miss its former abode –
A comfortable nest, with parental warmth?
Did it leave willingly, to move up north;
or was it fate's bequest – to set forth?
Were twigs dropping, signalling the fragility of the old
mortar?

Perhaps it was just unsafe for the fledgling to remain?

Sitting on a bench in the park;
I saw a tiny bird making a new nest –
In moments swift, it gathered nature's debris,
Beneath eucalyptus trees, a new home to be.
Will the new nest be as comfortable as its last?

Permanence

Like a marker on the school white board,
Unaware of its permanence, drawing eights and
capped parallel lines, bored.
The marks linger years on end,
In school tees with the same patterns, stories retold.

Hugs, a privilege, only mine to receive,
Breaking faucets, a shared mischief you believed.
Leaking tears, like a runny tap, unbridled intensity. You
first crush, best friend, life's whims we navigate.

In the bus, my scars and scratches, now faint and faded,
Two decades deep, like siblings, we've braided.
From school days shared, grade one to part to depart,
A phone call on my last day at home,
I just knew you'd call.

Curry Muncher

Curry, oh so yummy, you should try eating it with your hands,
get the sauce dripping, sliding down the side of your arms,

use your fingers, take some rice and mix it into a little ball,
Or scoop it with roti, whatever seems right.

The spice is nice, not just the heat but aromatics so fine!
Doesn't it smell of ghee, and garlic and ginger so divine?

No? Since you've boxed us in, let me share a secret –
You may think from north to south, we eat and speak the same –

Only once I left home did I learn curry was a flavour,
Packaged in small orange tins, far from what we savour.

Distilling my culture to the essence of curry powder's allure,
To foreign friends, your palates yet to fathom our culinary
lore.

Did you know that rasam whispers and tari hums in the
playground;
Amritsari chhole dance, its a melt-in-mouth delight profound!

Rajasthani daal-baati is arid sunlight's taste,
Rajma is my homecoming grace.

Marathi modak, a sweet treat from the heart,
Bengal's desserts, a love that sets apart.

Andhra's red chillies make North-East Indians sweat,
Spices, in unique proportions, each dish to beget.

Clove and cardamom perform kathak in pysam and kheer,
Beyond curry, a kingdom of aromas to revere.

Our food, more than curry, an orchestra of unique flavours.
For my culture, like our tongues, is rich and rare.

Every Fold...

Every fold, with care I hold.
I learn myself, and how much I cost -
how much of myself I must elude;
so I measure it with rolls of tape.
I caress it carefully, iron out the wrinkles of disrepute.
Flatten out the edges and tuck the corners,
smoothen the bedsheet over the firm mattress.
I need to merit love -
of others and of myself,
of my kin and their next.
So I thread the needle through and through,
Keep stitching the folds down.
Make sure there's no crease or rumple -
Every morning, I puff the pillows.
Every evening, I puff the pillows.
Take reckless paths with precarious slopes.

A Scorpion Sting

A Sisyphean journey to find myself -
I walked a wretched climb that steepened itself.
Sat atop a boulder to catch my breath,
A scorpion attacked me at the back of my legs.

I whimpered and cried,
It burnt my skin red and dry.
Itched and stung, that poisonous dart -
but it was my decision from the start.

It corrupted my soul, one prick at a time.
I yelled out curses which came back to me mimed.
The solo traveller lost with a swelling in the paw,
hadn't planned for this fatal flaw.

I took refuge in the cavernous cove -
beside winding path and tiring slopes
I lit a fire to keep myself warm,
And hoped the smoke would perhaps, inform?

In swarms, I hoped for days,
people would flock to help the one who went astray.
Slept around the the cold embers 'round the clock,
Yet no one came to my door and knocked.

Sweat dribbled down my forehead,
I sank deeper into my eternal bed.
Seventy two hours of hallucinogenic sleep -
I woke up parched and could barely breathe.

I looked around to see my body covered in rust,
Corroded beyond repair, was there no one I could trust?
I wriggled out and searched for something to quench my thirst
It wasn't something for which I had rehearsed.

I crawled out to the sea amongst the blue sky - the mighty sun,
Glowing in the distance, I wanted to chase after it, so I tried
to run.
The waves whispered tales of trials untold,
with each ebb and flow, a new story unfolds.

So, I continued on the journey to find myself -
I walked a wretched climb that steepened itself.

Blank Page

I'm scared of ink -
it leaches into the very fibre,
leaving a stain that I can't erase.

I try graphite instead -
but in hopes of it not being forgotten,
I frown to use it, too.

I try my luck with an assorted selection of words -
hoping the power of parol, leaves neither a blotch nor a
lasting hole,
alas, I might've ended up tearing a soul.

I try to weave a story with dye,
I yearn for its permanence to tell a tale -
hoping that it doesn't lose its way in translation.
Oh how often, I end up with a blank page.

Unworthy

In this wretched shell, ugliness resides,
Unattractive, grotesque, Nerdy, histrionic -
An excess of theatrics, a nauseating touch.
My skin, a map of despair, scalp's distress.
Inexperience, a stain, love's cruel lack.
Little, undeserving, piece of trash.
Struggling, destitute, life in disguise.
Too big, too small, a relentless torment.
Insecurities grip - You're bound to leave,
once you see past -
A people pleaser, fake loyalty's snare,
Holding hostages with deceptive care.
Unworthy of love in any guise,
Unworthy of any fight.
Through and through, a conniving, ugly self lies.

Everything feels like a movie...

Cheap wine, Smirnoff vodka.
Flickering yellow lights in the bathroom -
the smiling reflection in the mirror.
everything feels like a movie.
The terror,the fearlessness.
the horror, the delight.
the lights are dancing outside the door.
Card games we play, on the brink we teeter,
Nudging each other off the edge, it's getting sweeter.

Cheesy

2000s' rom-coms,
pick-up lines, cliches.
Autumn leaves,
horror movies in the darkness.
Scared walks across the river —
"darling, hold my hand!"
I loaned my jacket and draped it over you
on an icy winter evening,
hot chocolate, hot ramen.
Break my heart at the Greek Restaurant -
awkwardness so thick, you could cut it
with a knife. Running back into one another
on Valentine's Day. let's repeat it,
just for the plot. Leave each other,
once again, on a rainy evening in April.
Sure, keep calling me "cheesy"

A Caecilian

There is a caecilian, I think, that lives in my body,
It slithers through my skin and nestles in all my muscles.
It clenches! Makes me shiver, it gnaws at my lungs with might,
It anchors deep into the lining of my stomach, cutting through
like a blight.

My shoes bear witness to my body's struggle within,
Holes cut deep, where toes were meant to find peace.
Now I feel the ground, each step a test.
Jaws clenched at night, brown stained teeth in the morn,
A manifestation of a psyche well-worn.

I feel it around my ears, whispering in an amphibian language,
It is hard for me to decipher its needs,
does it need me to feed it something so it sleeps?
Or maybe a medicine that makes it leave for a bit,
but I doubt it will be easy to convince?

It wriggles around my brain, causing a convulsive itch.
Hard to explain - relations strained, trust elusive,
Every opportunity, a victim of my body's ailment.
A self-fulfilling prophecy, I am told, my perspective is unkind.
Beyond my brain, shroomy spores take flight,
Through the air, they shadow every light.

Bubbling Chai

I rest my head against the kitchen exhaust,
Watching the bubbling chai coming to a boil.
I lose myself in a daydream,
And think about how I'll be remembered—
Not by others, but by self,
Some forty years down the track.

The black tea leaves float to the surface,
And make me wonder of my pensive days in my rocking chair.
Will I remember myself to be kind and gentle?
A person there to help everyone,
Will I keep learning each day,
And hold onto compassion and love despite the heartbreak?

In spite of it all,
Will I be hopeful,
And be glad that I was—
For everything in the universe was nurturing me
with experiences to bear it all.
I hope I hold out my hand to save the drowning men
despite their betrayal.
Will I think of myself as handsome—
Despite my fatal flaws?

Or will I dive into sadness,
About not loving my body more?
Every tan line and stretch mark that painted me as a Tiger
Royale.
Will I have embraced it and worn it with pride?
Will I think that I was fun,
And that I still am?

Or will I be morose about the outcomes of things,
That happened in my youth,
And carry them forward like a dampened cloth?

Maverick

Setting a stage with a cinematic gaze,
I am enthralled by his tasteful embraces. I
Dive into his nutella-covered words.
Donning attires, quirky and brilliant, I look up to
Him, his style and his clever. We
Astral project, red eyed, into candy land of beautiful dreams.
Rhapsody enveloped adventures, fuel our vigour and glee.
Taking flight on whimsical tales, we soar so high,
He guides us both through galaxies with twinkling eyes.

Phone Call

Lucky moments, miracles,
The timing just works out right sometimes.
The presence,
The drives, in the afternoon and at three in the twilight.
The delay
of the plane, the train or the sunrise.
Just talk, let it out.
In person or over phone call,
At the right time, it saves lives
of a stranger or your best friend.

Belonging

Can't stop eating this creamy, dripping, white cheese Alfredo
sauce pasta,
the spicy 9-inch pizza freshly out of the oven,
yum, yum,
Can't stop pretending that I understand the
chitter-chatter, sitting on the table –
I quietly think about the pitter-patter
back in Melbourne, where rains pound the streets daily.
Pushing my rainbow umbrella away, turning it inside out, upside
down,
The gust, the blast, the gale, the puff
Of the big smoke, an amplified version of this town
I escaped, missing the warm hugs, I return each year,
I'm here, eating freshly baked pasta with them, feeling out of
place.
Unable to relate to the talks of their escapades
to even tinier towns, anymore,
I sulk, sigh, mope about my aloofness,
A lone quiet voice amongst the jabbering, gibberish, jumbled
words muttered about people –
I had known, do know, will know, I don't know?
Keep talking, I come here after a year, nothing to say,
How do I find things to talk to you about?
Nothing ever happens in Melbourne,
Everything happens in Melbourne, but not with me,
Things have been happening in Melbourne with me,
but the unspoken events linger awkwardly
sitting at the teak wood table as I listen, patiently,
Twirling tomatoey, gooey marinara spaghetti —
yum, yum.

Can I come back?

I think I'm falling out of love with you, ever so slightly,
It has been a while since I've caressed your face and
held you tightly. Each night, your heartbeat still calls,
Through the chaos and clutter, your presence enthrals.

I do miss your veins carrying memories of our playtime,
In your mouth, I've breathed the freshest air, amidst
the smoke that consumed me.
Your bosom has cradled my sadness, my grief.
In your womb, reborn a thousandfold I've been,
Moulting snakeskin -
Shedding layers, shedding pain, shedding despair, growing
inches -
Thrusting pain into your core, you bore it with grace.
Tolerating me despite my teenage angst, etched in
scorched marks on your golden hands.
Your hair, adorned with bougainvillaea vines, whispers tales
of our entwined romances.
In your embrace, I've felt both warmth and a jail.
I have been unknowingly pushing you away,
Breaking the bars and the shackles of pain.
Seeking comfort in transient affections.

Am I still entitled to the reliability of your embrace,
You were my longest love.
Have I taken you for granted, my home?
Like those battered men, having tasted the lips of countless
souls - return.
When all else fails, can I still come back to you?

Mango.

Am I?

Am I worse than those
Who commit crimes against the one who loves them the most?
Am I more wretched than the one
Who thrust the woman carrying his legacy into chaos,
Tossing her into the abyss of turmoil?
Am I more despicable than the one
Who skipped town only to have never returned?
Am I more vile than the one
Who, after battering his wife, paraded her exposed in the
marketplace,
Her body bruised in hues of red and blue?
Am I more repugnant than him
Who boldly declares intent to end his daughter's life for love?
Am I more abhorrent than she
Who veils her daughter-in-law in plain view,
Hiding her behind the same shroud she wore throughout her own
life?
Am I more contemptible than them
Who unheard their daughter's cries
And then beat their chest after she was set on fire?
Am I more wicked than the man
Who introduced another woman into his home,
Leaving the first to wither behind the earthen pot?
Am I more malevolent than the men
Who couldn't take no for an answer
For a moment's desperation, ripped out all her essence?
Am I more sinister than the man
Who tore his woman away from her parents
Because his honour eclipsed hers?

Yet, having witnessed these individuals celebrated by family
and society,
I ponder, why won't you, at the very least, acknowledge me.

Cheese & Crackers

First full time job,
second pay cheque.
Pending undergraduate dreams -
cheese & crackers,
some cold meats.
Charcuterie board.
Trivial things.
Hedonism.

Memo

I wish I got the memo for how to be at 15.
Guidance on trust, words to convey,
to those encircling me keen, helping me navigating life's
delicate themes,
To avoid the blunders that innocent love entices;
and to teach me to say, "no, I don't want to hear, I am just a
child!"

I wish I got the memo of what to do when you're 19,
Packing away your life, moving to different scenes.
A whisper, urging me not to clutch too tight,
Live like a student, revel in the night.
Beer-fueled laughter, acid-induced flights,
Enjoying fleeting connections, without binding rights.

I wish I got the memo of how you're supposed to feel at 22,
learning to embrace the fun of living as an adult. Despite
life swerving into another angle -
graduating, only to end up living in fear.
Hoping for a world less ruthless, not being locked away,
forgotten,
those first independent years not ending up in tears.

I wish I got the memo of what life is supposed to be at 23.
Yearning for guidance at adulthood's door,
Awakening, societal fucks to ignore.
Unlearning and realising, reality sets its tone,
Focusing less on society, more on the unknown.

I wish I get a memo, for each year of my life,
so I don't feel as lost or helpless as I did all this while.
And with that memo, I hope, comes a list
of instructions - a step-by-step manual
of how to assemble the pieces of life -
that autumn wind scattered around me.

Breathe

A message comes for me. I
break down immediately.
It seems bleak -
diminishing with every second the
light that I need.

Wings I didn't know I needed
before this moment. I
time travel into the future and
see my dreams come tumbling down.
Why?

A tiny thing affected my mind and my kin,
I think about it all the time, I
lock myself like they did themselves -
scared, jailed, take care;
breathless, sigh.

Cover up, don't breathe -
it spreads like bigotry.
Beating your innards like the boy that they did
yesterday, today, tomorrow
I just see -

Blood. Beep. Flush. Cough.
Repeat - until you can't. Until you don't.
Phone calls, pills, vermillion bottles, vitamins.
A drag of smoke, my lung's heavy with
the weight of my family.

Oceans between us. Prohibition stops us.
Friends that I need, a touch I can't feel.
Silent I sit. Green sheets,
Rumbling trees. Reality hits me like
The cold air they grasp for.

Even Charon Was Tired

In shadows cast by Charon's wearied oar,
Across the Styx, where souls drift ashore.
From homes to pyres, a sombre glide,
Where blood circles in an eternal tide.

Phelgethon's heat to the murky Ganges turned,
Souls emerged, to the banks they yearned.
Masses afloat, on funeral pyres
Crimson rose, amber skies.
Choking the city in ashy smoke.

Lethe's waters, where memories fade,
A son's grim act, a mother betrayed.
Stiff in a chair, breathless despair,
Oblivion's grasp, lunacy's hold.
A life wrapped up in a bag of toxic scum & thrown.

Acheron's waters, frozen in woe,
Flow into Delhi, a city aglow.
Holy waters, mingling with tears,
the world weeps, pilgrims dance around holy lakes.
The separation, the longing, enhancing fears.

Charon, tired, in Delhi's embrace,
Ferrying souls through time and space.
His lament, he couldn't no more –
Cocytus Banks where the homeless souls roam.

Dramatic

Contemplating a modest life turns my stomach,
I crave the dramatic - plot twists, struggles that define
A protagonist's fervent energy,
Simple love isn't my vision,
I fancy a fairytale romance,
A tragedy, clashing with kin,
Battle against foes. Brandishing swords. Vanquishing dragons,
Yearning for a grand romance, Itching for hurdles,
Obstacles strewn like petals in my path,
The snafu, spat, squabble, shindy;
A narrative arc that keeps my show interesting.
Exiled from my homeland's grace,
A longing for reconciliation,
Embraced by my chosen family,
Achilles heels and epic love.
Tip-toeing on a bridge, rescued by a stranger,
Who, in turn, falls deeply for me.
Sunlight piercing my eyes in a taxi's backseat
Orchestral symphony as background music.
A kiss before the credit's unfurling,
I'll bow to a standing ovation,
Waving as I say goodbye, taking
tangerine stairs up the sky.
I crave the dramatic, the untidy,
A saga, a folklore, an epic, a legacy.

Irony

Flourishing without an arm to hold onto,
In solitude, I languish.
Irony piles like the brown leaves on the broken pavement.
Autumn air carries with it more than just the remnants of
yesteryear -
a sullen coldness stings and
wraps me that even a yellow cardigan can't take away.
An icy shroud lay over my body each night,
That the mottled sunlight refuse to melt;
Eyes open, alert I sit -
Blue bedsheets, blue quilt, a lot more than just dead weight
surrounds me,
A grey blanket and grey pyjamas, grey ceiling and grey floor -
Turn me into stone I refute to be.
The more that I look, the less I see,
The more I seek, the less I perceive.
My heart aches for the unknown to me.

Melbourne

Roasted coffee, loose leaf tea, keep cups, recycled totes on the streets.
Enjoy the scenes, revel in curiosity, wobble head nods, inside mockery.
Bewitching sunsets, Beachside meanderings, late night spicy margs on the scene.
Espresso martinis, boogie on Smith, Rasputin!
Chilling in the pool, valley side cool, sundeck jamboree;
Chocolate treats, a fiesta queen, a parade of nations seen.
Arm chair nest, with woollen ball threads, her calm eyes gleam.

Two Garnets

He sat to string a necklace for himself,
One by one;
He passed precious stones
Through a golden thread.
Strung one by one, the pearls of Arabia,
Smoky Topaz and white jade from Korea.

He polished day and night,
Even sat for hours and chiselled away
The edges of his precious find.
He cut the souls of his precious gems
To carve an ornament beyond compare.

To create a centrepiece of his bejewelled thread,
He conjoined burning garnets into a golden shell,
Burning inside, a saturated sunset,
Fired by the air of our twin signs.

String it along, strung on a thread,
Two garnets on a golden thread,
Edged on either side by pearls of the midnight dive,
Until it caught ablaze by the red fire.

Jaded eyes held in itself the necklace that couldn't survive,
Shattering weeks and months of arduous strive.

If

If I was rich,
I'd travel across the globe's embrace.
Settle the debt that shadows my steps,
Bask in comfort's gentle beams,
And extend my arms to creatures in need,
Creating a sanctuary where care takes the lead.

If I wasn't tethered by societal norms,
I'd tread a path outside the expected forms,
Draped in attire both unique and true,
Breaking free from the fear of being oneself.
Foster relationships, with myself and them, that seamlessly
grow,
Nurture my mind and soul's vital health, (although that might
be a bit of a stretch.)

If my parents embrace me fully, as much as they think they do,
Our connection could bloom, unmarred by dispute,
Under one roof, tolerance could find a home,
I'd invite them into my world, no longer alone,
A bridge to understanding, love, and respect,
A journey together, a bond to perfect.

If I had the love of my life,
my mind would be calmer, my days a clear blue sky.
I wouldn't be as jealous of those around me.
I'd kiss them good night and wake them up with a kiss, (only
after brushing my teeth, that is.)
We'd sit in bed each morning, like my parents do, and catch up
on the news,
and at the dinner table, we'd chat about our day and topics
anew.

If I wasn't fat,
No more sucking in, no tight-shirt debate,
Unfazed by the clothing's numbered size.
In moments of intimacy, no more fumbling for the light switch.
Shirtless on the beach, I'd stride without any care,
I'd sprint towards the ocean's roar,
And perhaps, in the morning, I'd go for a run like those men by
the river shore.

If my skin were a shade that society might favour,
Chosen more by people of every colour,
Regardless of gender, more matches on apps,
Life experiences seeking my inner soul's maps,
Hired quickly, appreciated more,
Living a life that seems shiny and cool.

And if these "ifs" were to manifest,
Would I remain myself? Would poetry still flow from my pen?
Would true happiness find its home within me?
Would I be composing this verse?
What new "ifs" would then emerge?

Scary Business

Who lurks beyond the screen's veil of mystery?
A monstrous fool with sadistic thoughts,
or one with masochist undertones?
A bully, wielding standards far too high,
to shame, to judge with a merciless eye,
A lost soul, drunken, chasing highs untold -
With cocaine plastering their nasal sinuses,
Pills lining the kitchen sill like grapes,
In a fruit bowl of intoxicating escapes.
Or one who fetishises your skin, your words, your difference?
Perhaps a seeker of casual intimacy,
or an indifferent soul filling a gaping hole.

It's a scary business, I guess -
we'll find out.

Narcissist

Pantheonic King,
I sit high atop, the brightest and loudest
the prettiest –
with pools of paint, artistically drawn around my body
fashioned out of ambrosial milk,
and cream, boiling with nuts and spices so sweet –
almond, macademia and cinnamon speckles all over the skin,
Heavenly blood and mirth courses in my veins,
I forged myself, and you
and penned your destiny to serve my soul.
I'm the cosmic nucleus.
Your mercurial complications,
not as big as mine.
A pull so strong, I keep you in check –
you float around to satisfy my needs
encapsulating your entire world – me.
Navigating my whims, scripted to dispense at my wish.
Emotionless pawns in my tangled plot.
Side characters. Small, inconsequential
Not *Terra*, no mortal steps on my corse,
instead they fashion yellow sapphires, and wear it
around their fingers and neck
and pray looking at the night sky –
for soaring souls, justice they desired
an entry to the ninth heaven.
Bathed in the spotlight, I stand tall.
The brightest in the night sky.

Amber

Oh hello, Amber, hope you're doing alright;
Haven't seen you since that last party night.
Let's sit here under these rainbow lights -
I need to have a chat with you.

I've been feeling a little uncomfortable,
    and I've told my friends about it too -

You kiss me everytime we meet, then hold me close
and steer me towards the rooms and arms
that I'd rather not enter.
It's not that I don't have the agency, but -
        You haze my eyes, make my mind go round.
        Your beautiful face makes me guzzle my secrets out.

How do you do it?
        Stirring open -
                Confessions.
                Kisses
                Touches, from the depths of my soul,
                        that land me in a prison?
                Make me bare my soul to
                        my friends, acquaintances & foes.

                Wind me up
                        in unfamiliar beds.
                        In my bed with unfamiliar *thems*.
                        In my bed with an unfamiliar *self*.

        You put a mic in my hand - ask me to sing out loud.
        I entertained the crowd, and then passed out sound?
        Amber, you made a fool out of me.

I sigh.

Thinking of all the times -
        Lit-up summer evenings, Emerald & Sapphire dresses,
        Elegant twirls, Captured hurls, pani puris with a twist,
        Lopsided affairs, broken hearts, laughter shared with
        that girl you pushed me into.
        Oh, how the rejection came — it was funny
        but at least you were there to ease my pain.

Amber, remember that 90s party?
        Double-Denim attires came out, so did I.
        The first time I had, said it out loud,
        With no megaphone in hand, just Mel's ears and my voice,
        And then a kiss on your lips, good night!
        One of the only times I thought we were friends.

Stop whispering in my ears,
        my parents warned me about you.
        Hence, we never got to be friends when we were in school.
        But since we have mutual friends,
        we've got to keep it civil.
        I wish I could say we're friends,
        but friends don't treat each other the way we do.

And since I know I'll see you at the next party,
let's just stick to formalities?

Hookups

Awaiting stolen glances, elusive ownership in time,
Growing weary and tired, lost in the quest to find,
Substituting needs, entangled in transactional trysts.
No talk, just business –
Your skin, my skin,
Your lips on my dick.
For the passion and heat I crave,
The touch – so cold and bare.
Miles of silence stretch in this darkened room,
A paltry intimacy, an unspoken truth
Headboard croons its melancholic tune,
Filling me with pride, yet leaving me marooned.
Beneath the streetlights' flickering glow,
We play our games of hide and seek,
We find ourselves, but we never show, we never speak.
Chasing clandestine highs when desire peaks.

Marriages

On the account of the fact that, it is true,
I have not seen one good marriage,
I've resolved, almost subconsciously,
To shun commitment's entourage.

While not my original intention,
I've chosen fear as my provision,
Afraid of the concept of domestic,
I despise its very mention.

Movies depicting wedded bliss,
Evoke in me a mournful bark,
I think I'll encounter a similar fate,
The vows will bind me and weight will seal.

The white picket fences scream confinement,
A relentless assignment of suffocating expectations
I imagine a hip roof to crumble and close in on my soul.
Overwhelmed, consistently, toiling to meet familial
obligations.

In my thoughts, an austere undertones of life reveal –
in each house imprisoned, hearts let out a moan.
Every person, to me, cries nightly into their pillow.
Looking at the ceiling, regret, dreams of escape billow!

Sometimes, a yearning for companionship does stir,
Yet in an unfamiliar manner, it calls to me,
My heart confers to this novel concept,
It is different, far from what they see.

...but he does

She doesn't love me –

                                                but he does.

Her ways are a puzzle, complex,

                              He unravels, brings clarity, no pretext.

She bars the gates to my affection,

                              While he welcomes it, without objection.

She doesn't understand me,

                                      … but he does.

She has brought me hurt, time and time again,
Leaving scars, like an everlasting drought on the alluvial
plains.

        Winning her love feels like an elaborate mission,
With booby traps, secret bookshelves, escape room contrition –

                                  his, on the other hand, flows freely,
                   like a baby embracing its mother's teats, gently.

I await her love, longing to embrace her,
Offering reassurance, companionship, with a gentleman's ardour
–

I cling to hope for her tender touch,
                    yet find solace in his love, **a comforting clutch.**

Weary I grow – cherish his love because that's all I've ever
known.

        A meteor in the sky,
                    at least it makes itself visible to me.

Material

When I was just thirteen, I discovered a truth that was harsh
and unseen.
I wasn't desirable to the one I held dear, and our friend.
I discovered I wasn't fashioned to be suitable for
companionship.
Thus, my teenage years were plagued by self-doubt's grip.

Seemingly, we're all composed of a material,
Not chiffon, nor silk, not a fabric to alter,
But emotions that awaken and make others falter.
It wasn't my skin or the length of my lashes, nor

the hue of my eyes or my smile's perfect flashes.
It's because I evoke a feeling so damning, reduced to a
"brother",
As if a brother isn't a title honest enough,
I sulked and wept over the thought of their call

Years down the track I had a promotion of sort, it seems
My love and her friend cried over their broken hearts.
This time I rose in rank, and got promoted
to a material worth of being someone's husband. But

never a boyfriend, that's forbidden territory,
As if I couldn't elicit the shine they desired,never
captivating enough to be seen with lustful eyes,
I lacked the allure, the danger they sought.
Yet, I offered gentleness, care they were taught?

Over the years, I saw the pattern, repeating clear.
I had grown into my own, finding a different stance -
I drift in and out of that feeling but resolve, steadfast.
I knew my worth, deserving of love's tender advance.

Dirty Laundry

Dirty laundry piles,
the laundry basket keeps overflowing,
day in, day out
        White collared shirts,
                sweaty gym socks,
                        the cum-stained jocks
sneak beneath my bed despite
my meticulous laundering -
I persist in the wash,
the cycle keeps cycling like -
the lycra wearing middle-aged men riding to work,
every second day, unless it is raining.
peddling away.
The wheels keep wheeling -
an hour passes by.
I hang them on the rack in the living room,
Sweat beads on my forehead,
        trickles down my back,
                staining my freshly washed and worn clothes
in my colour and my smell.
My laundry basket had just emptied,
in a few hours time,
        my undergarments,
                my yellow stained t-shirt,
                        my blue sheets
will line the laundry basket,
awaiting their turn,
No matter how diligently I wash,
the dirty laundry keeps accumulating in mounds,
In the aquamarine laundry basket.

Youth

Artfully, characteristically queer, honing your uniqueness.
Brandishing confidence, your gaze so fearless;
I look up to you, lie next to you, envy your embrace of your
youth.
Relish your company, retire to sleep, realise my age and
question yours.

Representation

Brown skin, Turbaned men.
Educated, with or without the Indian accent.
Wrapped in kindness and flowers,
As sweet as peaches and mangoes.
Drenched in Blue, Pink and Purple light.

I fight with you in my sleep...

I want it back -
The years I spent fighting with myself -
In my sleep -
I dressed and undressed because -
I didn't like what I saw -
In the mirror a reflection -
Of a broken boy who didn't have -
Experiences of age,
Experiences of love,
Experiences belonging to the youth's prime;
Experiences lost, never found,
A life deferred, untold.
So now I am of age when people are experiencing -
experiences of age,
experiences of love,
the experience of commitment that I'm -
Too scared to jump into.
So I know I will repeat the melancholic note -
And fight with you in my dreams and when I am awake,
Every second of every day.

Goldfinch.

Seeds

I plough my garden bed, lay the groundwork with care.
The seeds germinate and give me a garden full of flowers
in the spring's tender air.

Spring

Two flat whites,
chilli scrambled eggs & tofu noodle salad.

a sticky pub floor,
a cider & a beer.

River front walks,
espresso martinis & mini golf jeers.

a missing yellow ball,
kisses next to the stadium & a freaked out stranger.

holding hands by the river,
a long walk & shared secrets.

pizzas with yoghurt,
rancid white wine & warm hugs.

early morning strolls back to the station,
shared showers & cuddled sleeps at your aunt's.

coffee al fresco,
Stars, Planets & us.

new haircuts,
shared photos & digs at each other.

Accidental matching,
coloured shirts & woes.

no pretense, just us,
at parties & in the elevators.

delayed Mexican dinner,
a scary night & confessions of exclusivity.

Cursed

Have you ever been trapped,
Bound to their side,
A slave to obligation?
Have you ever hesitated to sever ties,
Fearful of an old witch's curse,
A prophecy of doom and shattered support,
Leaving them to face fragments alone?
So you endure the pain,
Suppressing your essence,
Silent against their assault.
The old witch, triumphing, spells disaster,
Yet clinging to this only jeopardises your tomorrow.
Is it a curse upon them or upon you?

If I have loved you...

If I have loved you through what you've put me through,
will one aspect be enough for you to throw me in the trenches?
I stood by your side as my childhood was marred,
My innocence stolen, my face forever scarred.
Will my identity implode our bond, tear it apart,
Leaving behind fragments of a shattered heart?
Through snide remarks on my marks stretched and bare,
Will my existence alone shatter the fragile thread we share?
Doubting my origins, my connection to you,
Will you judge me unfairly?
I feel my fears coming true.

Mannik Singh| 26 |Goldfinch

Relate

"I know you want to, and do what you please,
this is still not the real world, where you're working the real deals,
But try to avoid drawing those smooth curvilinear lines,
Lest they'll become a habit and you won't be able to change.
Remember each stroke has to be built one day.
the walls you'll design will be very hard to manage.
So, if you want to avoid being called out –
Draw straight lines, at right angles, with care,
Where life flows easy, unmarred by blunder,
Beds fit snugly, to a standard measure."

You, my minder, you don't understand –
Drawing straight lines don't come easy,
I love the smoothness of the curves –
in shades of pinks and blues and purples,
I can't tone it to grayscale, I don't like it mellow.
Why don't you understand, there is an itch in my brain –
It skews even the straight,
softens harsh edges, blurs lines innate.

Him, my classmate, he did!
Saw me when I was struggling –
looking at a blank trace,
fixated to fit my teacher's demands,
paralysed, unable to move my pen
wanting to ace all their test, but not progressing,
wasting away hours, in my own head.
He held my hand, and helped me draw my lines,
even if I had to chuck some pages away, the progress was designed.
He showed his drawings, a booklet full of unrealistic designs –
and inspired!

I like curvilinear walls, you, my minder, proclaim they are impractical
but they're not to me.
To me, they're freedom, not laws to applaud.
Those standardised beds, uniform and bland,
Who'd settle for such when uniqueness is at hand?

and I am happy to design my own furniture –
Crafted to last, vibrant, and imbued.
If no one will build it, I'll happily do it myself.

But you, my minder, insist, persistently
You don't grasp my dilemmas, my mind's little tricks,
But I won't let your words bury me in bricks.
It's hard to understand things, I get it.
Why do you like black on white, I want to ask
and what's wrong with orange lines over green coloured card?
My minder doesn't understand, but I am not taking it to my
heart.

I don't remember not knowing you

In grey dungarees, on that first birthday,
A companion in a blue onesie, worlds away.
Who knew we'd meet on life's trains, crossing?

Travelling together, trials entwined,
Connected by fate, a bond designed.
A polaroid is constructed by time, no need to contemplate.

The first time you came over

You first visited amid October rains,
Bluestone paths washed, city lights aglow.
White flower petals marked our way home,
Their fragrance bound to memories - we'd forever know.

At 6:45, under station lights' soft gleam,
October's fifth night, a beautiful spring scene.
Eyes met, hearts raced, anticipation hung,
I yearned for you to recall this moment young.

The corner restaurant buzzed with life,
While the café stood silent, serene.
My heart was happy, excited and equally scared
Of you seeing my life that I'd hoped you'd share.

Unfurling for the first time, for me, was a tale I'd hoped –
All my life, I had begged for and cursed.
We shared that evening, with wine and a friend;
In the night, however, it was just us, without pretend.

No way, you're mine!
No way, you're mine?

Vow

On the black couch, you slept next to me,
In your black T, you clung to me
Drifted off as the credits gracefully unfurled,
Just slept, a silent moment, nothing hurled.

It was the first time we lay down next to one another.
I drew you close, tousled your chestnut locks.
Before knowing your birthdate, or the stars' sway,
I sensed I'd stir mac n cheese at 3AM, share nights and days.

I'd gift you the cool side of pillows, warm our bed,
Watch films undistracted, horror too, without dread,
I'd forgo cruises, dwell on the first floor's view, for you.
All for the promise of a life with you.

And as cliche as it is,
promised to bestow upon you the universe and beyond.
Vowed, months later, to you as we were drifting off to sleep,
to make you the happiest person in this whole world.

Peering through the Window

Kindly knitting sweaters, glasses perched on your nose,
Orange peels peeled, your messy hair in a bun.
Mittens holding a warm teacup, your favourite book close.
A lovely golden hour peering through the window, as we
Lounge in our living room.

New York

My lover and I have talked.
We want to live in New York.
On the first floor, above a rustic Jewish cafe,
perhaps in West Village,
ride down Central Park, party on the East Side.

My friend and I have talked,
We want to live in New York.
Open a bespoke architecture firm on the Brooklyn shore,
sip on lattes and walk by the Hudson River,
sketch beautiful landscapes; the ones we saw in books.

And I, with thoughts that oft arise,
Long for New York in my writer's eyes,
On the first floor, above a bookshop aged,
From the 1900s, a timeless page.
I'll perch at my window, half-leg dangling free,
And pen beautiful prose.

Bored

Soon enough you'll be bored of me -
Of my deceiving gazes, my actions and the countless attempts
of reinvention
Such is fate, predestined in the silver linings of the dark
clouds,
that I cannot blow away.

You'll tolerate my company until a shiny dandy reveals life in
fresher hues,
My smile will lie defeated in your lap one last time -
The ocean we gazed into, will come streaming through my eyes,
and our memories will morph into bullets that shoot in my hurt.

Before long, you'll grow weary of me,
Hence, I persist, for as long as possible.
Striving to be more captivating, constantly evolving, the
finest!
Someone to showcase, someone you're proud to embrace.

So, I will keep pushing myself to do things, that I think
you'll desire -
put myself in positions that I know will satisfy you.
I am right down in it, accepting it as a challenge.

On the day you tire of me,
may you recognise my pain, communicate, and then depart, please
as gracefully as you arrived, without leaving me blindsided.
Promise me, don't be behind the gun that will kill me
prematurely.

My Life at 25

My life at twenty-five –
A handful of chosen friends,
Navigating with me through the obstacles in a pinball machine.
Some left behind in obsidian crannies,
Others join me in my ocean of melancholy.

My life at twenty-five –
An idea of home that isn't concrete and brick,
Nor is it made of timber beams.
My home eludes familiarity,
A place where I struggle to be.

My life at twenty-five –
I have the one who cares for me,
Only just enough to stop me bleed.
Am I not deserving to be loved with passion and a heat that
inspires?
Or am I destined to be just another fleeting smile?

My life at twenty-five,
A train journey, racing past life's stripes.
Blanket faces on blue attires.
Excelling at making a living of life.
Curating experiences for someone else to thrive.

Barter

I didn't want it to be a barter,
Oh, love like this I hadn't chartered.

In this delicate dance of hearts we tread,
Hoping for a love that is freely spread.

But love's nature, it seems, can be a riddle,
To be loved just a little, an unexpected middle.

I stand now, with a bitter sweet sigh,
Realising love's uneven supply.

In my mind, this lesson I'll keep,
To love someone fully, doesn't guarantee love's leap.

Five AM

At five am,
My grey ghost sits on the window sill and hopes for the sun to
come out and shine.
It pines for the filtered light to melt the frigidity –
That the midnight sky plastered me in.

My grey ghost floats in space,
Dances in the white light of the refrigerator and
Sits on the sofa in the living room looking out into the
distance
the ember rays are yet to be gained.

My grey ghost stands against the cabinet containing my mother's
favourite tea set watching
The trees in the distance over the horizon, dance in harmony.
Their Viridian mixed with Prussian of the Stygian sky
Disturbing each stroke of the Starry Night.

My grey ghost swings on my grandmothers rocking chair –
Ticking wall clock and buzz of loose wiring traversing through
its gossamer veil.
Day old Tea in the grey cup beside the chair turning hoary.
Misty window panes pain.

My grey ghost paces from room to room with trembling sighs.
The tap in the bathroom dripping at regular intervals making it
cry.
It pauses over my cold body and tries to jolt it awake.
Alas, no one can be brought out of a cadaverous state.

My grey ghost lies next to me
With Frosty eye lashes, saxe head tilted to side.
It caresses my fluttering eyelids and scars on my face,
Beside my case, he gives me a smile.
My grey ghosts and I
Waiting for golden rays at five AM.

Wedding Bath

Prepare the *Vatna*, rub it in deep—
cleanse her skin of every impurity.
The mustard and turmeric paste,
we work it in, scrubbing until every hair
is gone—she glows now, vibrant,
bathed in golden light.

Kachi Lassi, rose petals
in a marble bathtub. She is beautiful -
so pure, untouched.
Let her simmer in that steam,
prepare her for her husband -
radiant, opulent. Make her face ambrosial.
She looks so heavenly! I love how
her tears fill the bathtub,
how happy she must be!
But it won't overflow.
It is diluting the milk even more -
and we put more rose petals,
maybe some rose water -
perfume her aura, sincere.
Wash her
of her sins, tongues she touched,
words she mouthed -
only for her future dear.
We braid her hair, and let her sit
alone, just a bit —
and when the time is right,
we'll pat her dry, and prepare her for life.

Longing

Longing extended stares, robbed visions, my gaze -
                              his property,
Your pink smile with white tiles, soccer queen dreams. It seems
                    as though a
Decade had passed staring into your stable ground,
                         leather book eyes,
I hold back, look away, lingering thoughts, a tangled maze -
Aching for your touch, a second of your embrace.

A Reason

Worst best times,
Best worst crimes.
I search for a reason -
Hoping there will be some treason.

Civil war rages;
Battles waged, my nation enrages.
Amongst the fallen concrete stages, the only cold that stings
is yours;
shudder- despite the warmth of our burning string, I cling to
myself evermore.

The battleships lowered their cannons.
Half hearted Treaties came, but they are better than none?
I throw matches, hoping fire catches,
But we dance through the fury crashes.

In the wake of heinous deeds, I strive -
To find some twisted solace, to keep this fight alive.
Alas, no reason to expose - not a secret to unveil, nor a
strife.
So I continue, fuelled by rage and defiance -
In this never-ending quest for my own reliance.

Dry Choices

Winter winds had dried up my dreams –
August lapsed away and the next is on my door steps it seems.
Memories rush back to me, carried on the breeze.
When I saw your smile, my heart found at unease.

Running into you, was it fate's subtle hand?
An accidental meeting to help me forget what's mine?
In that moment, time stood still suspended,
As if the universe conspired, and our paths blended.

I stood there at the station platform of choice.
Undecided – what train to take – one that's real or one I long
to rejoice?
Should I hold onto these stolen moments, fleeting
Or release them like the snow, melting and receding?

Why I don't...

There's a reason why
I don't tell you
that,
It does bring me down -
that,
This heavy weight is a painful
frown,
that,
silence remains, my only gown.

There's a reason why
I don't tell you
that,
I feel like I am an imposition
-
that
I feel I'm a burden, a constant
intrusion,
that,
I yearn for a loving
resolution.

There's a reason why
I don't tell you
that,
It tires me so much to request
-
that,
My pleas unheard makes my heart
distressed,
that,
This weariness grows, my soul
oppressed.

There's a reason why
I don't tell you
that,
It hurts me every single time
you overlook my hurt -
that,
My wounds ignored are left to
covertly spurt,
that,
I ache for empathy, for
understanding, not inert.

There's a reason why
I don't tell you
that,
I want to stop loving you -
that,
I want to break the chains and
bid adieu,
that,
Despite all, my love lingers,
stubborn and true.

There's a reason why
I don't tell you
that,
It hurts me that you don't -
that,
My love unrequited is a painful
font,
that
I crave reciprocation, a love
that won't taunt.

There's a reason why
I don't tell you
that,
Giving you all my best, brings
out the worst in me -
that,
It's a paradox, a painful decree,
that,
I yearn to be free, to finally
see.

There's a reason why
I don't tell you
that,
I want you to put an end to this
-
that
I want you to acknowledge the
pain, grant me bliss,
that,
I want you to release me from
this abyss.

Why does no one see?

How do I show you
how I -
Stay up,
        work late,
                days on end?
Why do these tired eyes go unnoticed?
Can't you see the etched scars of countless nights?
My back bent, like tired parched branches bowed
with the weight of red autumn leaves,
        my neck strained under the burden of relentless toil.

A casualty of trying to be someone,
Working under pressure, acing tests strewn for me,
Working out, keeping fit, cooking meals, cleaning,
always busy,
        always broke,
                always on the edge,
Away from familiarity, away from loved one's embrace
after a hard day at work
No one to say "You did well, come, have a seat,"
Set the dinner table with a simple meal.

Every night, I continue.
Pushing aside the fear of wilting,
A sunflower!
I persevere in the twilight.
I swear, I believe I've earned the recognition.
Though I may hide,
                I'm aware of my worth.
It stings
To elude the honour I pursue,
                For myself and my family.

What do I do differently,
To gain your validity?

Calm

Yesterday, you said something that soothed my soul,
Yesterday you said, "in a world that's out there to
                            make me angry and scared,
                                        You calm me."

And somehow,
You knew what to say.
Just as my faith was beginning to wane —
                            "You calmed me, too."

                                        29/06/2023

High

In wisps of smoke, clarity unfolds,
Beneath moon's gaze through your window's hold.
Guide me into the now, with you alone,
Just us, our lips.
Pulsating bodies never felt this serene.
You on your grey sofa, me, poised in contemplation,
Praising the divine for how good it feels!
Eyes sealed, tongue bathed in anticipation.
A languid moan, a duet in hushed cadence,
All our senses so aware yet calm.
Crimson wine, a sweet cascade down my throat.

A Nod

You nodded and said the unsaid.
I decided then –
I'll stay.

You said the words.
And I decided then –
I'll be with you until it destroys me.

08/07/2023

Pull

Starry vision in your eyes, meticulously crafted in the
Onyx skies, with moon shine over the obsidian mountains side.
Haze of fog, your brain's treacherous talk, I'd hold on to you,
And pull you up from the steep valley slopes, carrying your
                    burden as we carry on our
Nightly toll, waiting for the dawn.

Mannik Singh| 26 |Goldfinch

Stranded

I feel as though I've been stranded.
Oceans stretch between my dreams and fate,
Forging new life, seems oh how futile!
My hope dims for another dawn's embrace.

The ocean keeps rising, or does my island sink with time?
Who knows if this land will stand against the motions that
rhyme?
Will I rise above the waves or sink, bound by heavy chains?
I feel this tsunami will destroy everything I've built;
it will take promises I've vowed to keep -
and bury them like treasure unfulfilled beneath the ocean bed.

Foes and friends on distant shores,
Seem to have forgotten my laughter's strains.
Even If I surf over these waves, reclaim my homeland's grace,
they'll treat me like an alien from outer space.
At least in these foreign lands, my smile has broadened,
it doesn't hide behind a masquerade attire.
Within these motions, however, it's beginning to wane.

I feel as though I'm stranded.
Messages in bottle, adrift, unanswered still-
None of the choices in front of me right or just.
A life jacket, in a stranger's hands.
Will they trust me, and throw it my way?
Or will they let me fall from grace's hill?

Isolation's grip, a relentless, enduring chill,
In its clutches, I remain stranded still.

Richmond Dreams

We're bound for the UK's embrace,
If my time wanes in this space,
Perhaps, in my hometown's grace, I'll sit tight,
Awaiting our future's subtle chime.

You vowed, we'll make it work, and
Crafted beautiful visions in my eyes.
We'll travel to your hometown in May, June, July.
When the weather is just so fine!

Meet your friends under starry light,
Uncover tales of your teenage nights.
Nightly, you'll toil as I explore your history, while every
morning –
we travel everywhere you've been, on this island of yours.

You said, I'll have to go to the old smoke alone,
Ah, London, a city you disdain, yet with a nudge,
You surrendered, saying, "Fine," with a gentle judge.
I rolled my eyes, and quietly said, I won!

And then in Manchester, the city you hold so dear,
You'll grip my hand extra tight, with so much joy and cheer!
Edinburgh is a must, you proclaimed with glee,
And to the south of England, where shores are very pretty.

And while we await our future call,
We'll sip coffee, sitting in Richmond.

Intoxicated

Just, under the moonlit skies, your wolven eyes, high on drugs
                              undefined -
And alcohol, tequila smoke veiling your soul.
Mine, staring into the depth of yours -
Embracing your pupils' dilation, enchanting my
Soul and taking over my body's hold.

Satanist

Your butt, so cute, I said with a grin,
What earned you such a cushion, so soft within?
You replied, with a chuckle, in a tone quite chill,
"I sold my soul to Satan, I guess that's the deal."

Love Leak

My love,
The scale keeps circling,
Round and round,
Like my cheeks
that my friends say
have become spherical.
They whisper
I'm keeping secrets,
like I've stuffed
chubby bunnies,
like squirrels hoard nuts
in their mouth pouches.
Rich, fatty, gorgeous, cute,
Marshmallow sweet,
Pink and white and caramel brown.

I'm spilling, spreading -
pouring from my lips
gargling, spitting up.
Moscato sweet, Grenache deep
wine staining my bed.
My stomach spills over,
droops past my waistband.
I tuck it inside,
Hide it from neighbours' sight,
Fearing their judgement, their evil eye.

My jeans rip at the seams
like tears down my face,
watching debonair couples hand in hand
on city streets,
on tiny screens,
across oceans I can't swim.

I am splashing slopping, sloshing
Bending, brimming, ruining my posture to conceal
the warm, soft cushion
taped around my chest.

My love, I am leaking,
I think they can tell—
How do I hide it?
(I don't want to hide it)

Tuesdays

Like my hands around your face, I embrace Tuesdays tight,
No need to withhold breath or tense my gut; with you and our wine,
Knowing you're mine tonight, I exclaim with delight, *Wild nights - Wild nights!*

All day I labour with a smile, knowing evening brings your sight,
In jest, I hold you close as you stir the sauce - *savoury sage, rosemary, and thyme.*
Like a gentle embrace around your waist, I hold Tuesdays tight.

Your passion is my inspiration, your ethics are my guiding light;
In the reflections as we drift into sleep, you unfold a lifetime,
Knowing you're mine tonight, I exclaim with delight, *Wild nights - Wild nights!*

Bickering over the home we'll share in wedded bliss, my face grows bright,
I've got nothing to fear, on the last page you are mine, my love, you are mine!
Like my arms around your frame, I embrace Tuesdays tight!

We'll argue over life and forget it on Wednesday morning, regardless of our fights -
I'll bring warm chicken soup to you, when you're sick and in wintertime.
Like my hands around your face, I embrace Tuesdays tight,
Knowing you're mine tonight, I exclaim with delight, *Wild nights - Wild nights!*

**Emily Dickinson's - Wild Nights! Wild Nights!*
Frank Kidson - Scarborough Fair

Tangerine.

Finally!

It was finally my time to launch upwards and onwards
towards the moons and stars, to travel galaxies beyond
the visions of those in my small hometown.

My black cape was ironed, my helmet and black suit was ready.
Full throttle, the power, the might.
Visions of accelerating, leaving behind troubles of a stressful
life.

Sacred promises of a lovely time,
my partner by my side, a mission at hand.
The people in the control station, ready to countdown.

1...2...3...Ignition!
The smoke billowed, like a freight train or a ship,
Carrying my dreams, sinking like the *Loch Ard* in the misty
rain.

My spacecraft failed to launch,
Despite the labour and fuel,
Despite my meticulous calculations of risks and errors.

Amidst the dissipating haze, my fellow traveller was gone,
the controllers stood in their tower, shrugged and went off to
lunch.
And I sat, in the cockpit, tethered to the ground.
What just happened?

You kicked me out

You kicked me out, a ticking time bomb of betrayal
In the echoes of shattered trust, our love began to flail.
Pain, guilt, impending doom in a haze of confusion,
For the first time, the one who brought me calm - scared me.
I was startled and needed saving.

Departing in search of solace, a tequila bottle in hand,
Alone on the curb amidst a thunderstorm
I sat, its contents to unwind.
Before I called a cab and then I cried because
I didn't want it to end - neither the alcohol nor our bond,
lost between my infidelity and the wounds you gave me to mend.

As the sun emerged, a witness to my remorse,
Failing to face the rays, I turned down the blinds -
shielding my shame, regret took its course
I couldn't bear to see myself and the devastation around -
The alarm's harsh sound jolted me awake
some 10 hours down the track -

through the workday, I pondered, a soul in heartache.
Reflections on where it all went astray.
In the debris of love, we both are left to fret.
I yearned to assign blame, to point the accusing finger -
Yet, within myself, I realised, patterns lingered.

Internal apologies whispered, though I knew
they couldn't mend the damage, neither me nor you.
I, a human bomb, detonated, the aftermath severe -
Self-destruction wrought, and you held dear.

Running through an empty hospital

I ran through an empty hospital -
With no sound but my heartbeat in my ears.
I kept looking for you to sit down and talk
and mend the things that you broke;
And I broke down.
An hour passed in futile exploration—
Down lifeless corridors, fatigue clung to my steps.
I exhaled weariness,
Unable to find you,
Helplessness lingered.
I meandered aimlessly,
Despite seeing your face in strangers disposition
in the foyer, in the cafeteria.
I waved, nothing came back to me mimed.
Upon closer inspection, they weren't mine.
A text unreceived, so I sent one tied to a messenger pigeon -
He came back with "I need time",
What time?

A ~~Reason~~ Lifetime

I wish you were a lifetime,
Not *"a reason"* as they all say.
I could harbour hatred for your deeds,
Yet gratitude emerges instead —
For being my first "everything".

The palette of opinions about you may be diverse, yet those
colours belonged uniquely to us.
Your hues, a blend of blue and red,
Became my own, indelibly etched.
And I will spend a lifetime trying to wash them away -
Struggling until the reminder wanes.
Striving until the indigo fades,
and I discover I've become purple -
Deep and opulent,
Like your favourite colour.

I wish you were a lifetime,
And you were, however, an ephemeral chapter of fourteen moons.
Unveiling new worlds, my ethereal monsoon -
Growing green life over my once barren ground.

I could harbour hate, for valid reasons,
Yet love lingers, the reason not to.

...well, we are here now

…well, we are here now
You sit before me,
Eyes evading mine like butterflies flitting between distractions in
a Mexican tapas bar —
the colourful boxes, bottles of alcohol
and a bartender that wouldn't serve us

I yearn for words to flow between us,
An exchange of questions and raw confessions.
My heart, a battlefield, longs for acknowledgment,
For the pain you've sown, an avalanche of emotions,
Crashing into sleepless, starless nights.

I looked inward to find ways to talk to you.
I had a running list of conversations and questions and anecdotes
I wished to talk to you about,
Another list of things that I wanted to say to you, call you and
scream in your face.

I wanted to ask you questions about what went wrong and when.
I wanted to ask you about your day,
I wanted to ask if your employer still plays the role of the
relentless dickhead.
To share the irrelevant annoyance of my flatmate,
Unravel the layers of emotions post-you, post-us.

I wanted to tell you about the new song I discovered while trying
to get over you
I wanted to tell you that I can't listen to my favourite songs
the same anymore
The pain of melodies tainted by your absence.
I wished to thank you for facilitating relatability to songs I
had always loved

More blame I wanted to unleash at you
Insomnia's grip, appetite's departure,
My sullen face in celebrations, weddings and the places that
charged us.
I yearned for your acknowledgment for your part in all of this,
I wanted you to fight with me and say it was my fault too.

Spoiled by romcoms of the 2000s, I sought a cinematic resolution,
I wanted you to tell me that somehow, our broken hearts can be
mended too -

A grand gesture, a whiteboard outside my door with apologetic
words written in deep purple.
How long would your disloyalty have endured if not caught red-
handed?
Did your blue-blooded betrayal consider my warm orange?

We spoke, diving into the deepest depths after a turbulent fifteen
minutes,
Confusion lingering, tears swelling in both our eyes.
The air around us stifled our screams,
A debate over whether returning is worth the risk,
Or if we're destined for a worse fate six months hence.

Is it different from the unspeakable truths,
A contract signed in the early days of dating,
Culminating in "I do" or a fiery demise?
A bet I hoped you'd take, fighting your demons and the shame.

I begged you to fix this once and for all,
Laying my vulnerabilities on the table,
But the tables turned, now you the victim.
Internally screaming, "I was the one wronged,
The one you should've fought for,
The one you should've begged for."

As we grapple with the fallout,
I confront the blurred lines of truth and deception,
Haunted by a year marred by shadows of deceit.
The shattered trust, a puzzle to reassemble,
Can it be pieced together again?

Oh, what have you done to me?

Now, we stand outside your home,
I linger, an eternal outsider, begging entry,
Yearning to cleanse the mess that binds us.
Amidst confusion, sadness veils my desires,
Leaving me adrift, searching for clarity.

What do I truly want?
The answer eludes me, obscured by the fog of sorrow.
A silent plea persists—to rediscover the 'us' we once were,
Preferably together
If not, content in our separate solitudes.

Panic Attack

Exhale! Inhale! Exhale! Inhale!
Why? How? What if I had? What if you...?
Black and white, fire and dance.
Head under the ocean, only rivulets on my pillow.

Exhale!
In the midst of some kind of panic attack, what is the remedy?
In the echo of your plea for space,
amid the chaos within your mind,
I would have offered you the expanse of the earth,
cleared paths for you to find.
But, I couldn't let you face solitude,
watch you shiver in the cold alone.
Should I have left you to be on your own?
Instead of holding your hands, dropping you home?

Inhale!
What triggered the panic –
Did the realisation finally creep up your legs?
Did you finally catch up with your betrayal?
Did you finally have something real – that startled your senses?
I'm sure you're fine, *I don't think you even realise –*
how much it shook me for you –
to say you love me, knowing it was untrue;
to say you wanted to fix things, and realised you didn't have
in you?

Exhale!
Since *you're fine, now,* and I'm not – can you tell me?
How did my touch not soothe your soul?
If the tables were turned, I'd have simply slithered into
sleep.
Did you take deep breaths with lavender near your nose?
or was it another drug?
What was the object that you focused on;
Perhaps a new subject, who brought you calm?

Exhale!
But when you threw acids of blame in my face,
Realisation struck, we differ in expression and expectation.
I am ashamed for clinging, unwilling to let you part,
for *hugging, kissing,* fearing the unknown,
not letting you depart.

Inhale
Take all the space, to calm your nerves –
"I had another panic attack about it yesterday,"
and I've been saying this for months, too.
Believing I did right, I stand corrected now,
Amid accusations, I wonder about my plight,
My desire to breathe new life into this, stifled.

      but you need to hold;
      slowly exhale.
      Repeat, when the next wave comes.

Cognitive Dissonance

It is red, it is blue
The cold stings, I found warmth, too
A paradox, unsettling sway,

I trust in gold, I trust in tangerine
Generously cunning and deceptive, stingy only on bad days
Beliefs at odds, a turbulent dance,

A home, my nest, my repose
Elegant Twigs, views encaged
A clash of ideas, like waves on the shore,

Beautiful butterfly, no, an unsightly moth
A rose garden with lush bushes, a forbidden barren plot
The heart believes, the mind denies,

A fragile balance, teetering on the edge,
Reason and belief, a contentious wedge
What is the truth? Did I just imagine it all?

Things I did trying to get over you

Cried,
Told my friends about what you did –
Not just that once, over the year of our time.
Questioned my worth, doubted our love's birth.
Sceptical of shared moments, in doubts I dove –
Cried overseas, Bangkok held my woes.
Smiled bright at weddings, an Oscar-worthy pose.
Listened to Gracie Abrams and Taylor Swift,
Now I realise why they sang it like they did.
Stood in front of the mirror at 3AM, slapped myself for missing
you after what you did.
Threw up and fell sick.
Deleted our shared note beneath a lonely moon.
Masturbated, tears kept their flow.
Failed to hookup with some stranger, what a shame!
Stalked you on the same hook up apps, seeking signs of your
indifferent move.
Tried looking at blurry faces on dating apps, no care.
Read poetry, wrote some in the groove.
Masturbated thinking about our time.
Tarot Card readings on Instagram, delusions amassed.
Burned Chillis to cast off the evil eye,
Even the ritual of cleansing my soul with salt transpired.
Cried endlessly, ate nothing all day;
Emptied the fridge one sorrowful night's sway.
Called and blamed, interrogated in vain,
Begged for your return, met silence's disdain.
Cried when you didn't fight.
Cried when you requested some space and no sight.
Showered away traces of your touch.
Laundry to cleanse, your scents to clutch.
Emily Dickinson and trashy comedies, a strange mix!
Cried with friends, sister, in loneliness's fix.
Cuddled a pillow, a surrogate for you.
I could take to drugs or some alcohol, a fleeting solace sought –
Oh damn! What an expensive thought!
Decided to take a bath and wrote this shitty poem.

30/12/2023

Spark

At times, we're trapped within our frame,
Between ribs' confines, where no light pours in.
Is there still a shiny lustre to our soul,
Is there a heart that's still pumping the warm-warm gold?

Sometimes, pain drills through our cerebral plains,
We scream and cry and yell and fight against the strains,
but find ourselves helpless in whatever we may try.
Bursting our lungs and corrupting our blood;
we often become as harsh as the winter weather.

We wait and long for a flickering flame,
To thaw this cold-cold frost over ourselves
and release us from the tame.

Does it feel like that this is our time?
Carrying on seems futile,
Yet, with every atom of our remaining consciousness,
We seek solace in someone who can pacify
The afflictions that haunt, until darkness is nigh.

Kill the Hope

In surrendering control,
I'll pirouette on
and on the escarpment terrain,
I'll be a silhouette
caressing the nape of his neck-
flinging forward towards the edge,
ready to soar like a gull.
I'll leap from the Cape Schanck cliffs,
down into the ocean's depths,
I'll pretend I know how to swim.
If the tides shove me against the jagged shores,
where blood might seep from my skin.
I'll happily lose control and vanish away.
If I drown, I'll let my lungs fill with salt water,
Should someone rescue me in time, and pump the water out,
I'll remember being flooded by the draws
I once took from your silver pipe
exhale the salt, like smoke.
I cough. I cough. I cough.
Hoping in this quest, they're able to expunge
every ounce of this hope.

Mannik Singh| 26 |Tangerine

Ghosts from the Halloween night
Have been scaring me in my dreams the past 2 months.
It's almost February.

Dodge & Chase

I took a walk today, down to the river
where, each summer, this bar extends onto the river
on a floating island. Quirky Capitalism. I thought
you had vowed to bring down capitalism and how you
hated everything it stood for, but this was your
favourite place in the city. I guess I should've known
how you failed to act on things you held so high,
your moral compass
always aligning truth, your words not mine.

So I went searching for you, along the bank, hoping
to catch a glimpse of you on that Monday afternoon when
you had time off work. It was sunny, I was wearing my sunnies,
hands
in the pocket, walking nonchalantly, as if. To my relief I
didn't see you,
even when I went searching for you. I'm a masochist.
I love seeing myself in pain, being trapped, needing to think
on my feet.

I think you and I are alike in this,
contradicting everything we believe in. I wonder
what were your constraints, to justify your actions. What was
your approach to ethics and your own philosophy?
Did you employ the scientific method in your quest? Or were your
actions guided by a different zest?
For a philosopher, you weren't very kind to me – rather
ruthlessly you destroyed my sense of self, made me act unlike
myself.
You let me believe, even after I told you,
that I was losing my mind over things I felt.
It's all good though, I guess?

Despite it all, I find myself taking lunchtime walks,
Hoping to stumble upon you, chasing shadows that resemble you.
Running after names that sound like yours (why do you have such
a common name?).
When I glimpse your hair, your burgundy T-shirt on someone
else,
I dodge their gaze, fleeing from echoes of you,
Avoiding those who remind me of you,
In actions, in words, in essence, you.
We're alike, you and I.

Confession.

Your Honour,

This is a sworn statement of mine, that I am freely and
voluntarily giving to you. I'm surrendering myself, and with
that I hand into evidence my insecurities, my wrongdoings, and
my role in the murder of our relationship.

I'll hand out the transcripts of the lengthy messages, if you
have chosen to delete them, just to refresh the memory, should
you wish to entertain the evidences of this crime. With that
I'll hand to you the photographs, of us frozen in love. From
our shared trips, our dates, kisses and dinners. In case you'd
forgotten that we were in love.

To start, I regret the dust-storms of words, the blindside
assaults on your senses. Leaving you blinded, time and
time again. I wish I had been more patient with our love;
explanation, I withheld — my hurt, my needs, my dreams. I wish
I had taken more time to help you learn how to love the way I
want to be loved.

I willingly confess to coercing you into this union, providing
no alternative but an ultimatum—a tragic choice between leaving
or uttering three words. I should have allowed you to navigate
at your pace, granting you a voice to avert this chaos.

Time ticking, morphing into doubts, suspicions of your
infidelity. My mind, a playground of fears, drove me to seek
you in strangers' faces, in nameless souls, faceless torsos,
in barren tiles. Love, once showered to bind you, laced with
sweetness undesired, every word coaxed with sugar and honey.
I failed to heed your palate, your distaste for saccharine
promises.

Space and time, commodities I denied you. My fears drove
demands for attention, meetings, a weekly ritual imposed. I
acknowledge the unfairness, the folly of binding you while
you sought independence in a new city. Apologies, belated and
sincere, for the imposition and the ignorance.

I wish I were more grateful for every single good thing you did
You never imposed or coerced me into being someone I wasn't
or into attempting something I wasn't prepared for. I should
have treasured and cherished you more deeply, far beyond what
I managed. I wish I had expressed gratitude for every morning
coffee you brewed,and every shared glass of wine in the
evenings. Now, all I can offer are apologies for failing to
appreciate you and all your efforts. Perhaps if I had been more
appreciative, we wouldn't be in this position.

Deepest remorse now surfaces for my failure to understand your
mind, the neural pathways hidden in darkness. Your attempts to
explain, lost in translation. I questioned whether your mental
health constrained our love or if you simply chose not to give
more. Apologies resonate for misconceptions, subconscious self-
sabotage, for not being patient with your mind.

Finally, deepest regret for the unleashed anger, a punch to
your arm, staining our last night. It haunts me, a momentary
lapse in control fueled by emotions. I swear not to be an
angry person, a casualty of proof of betrayal. I've tortured
myself as penance, acknowledging it might have sealed our fate.

In conclusion, Your Honour, I humbly submit this confession
as a testament to my remorse and regret, understanding the
gravity of my confessions. I willingly lay bare the flaws and
shortcomings that contributed to the demise of our love. <u>I
eagerly await, your judgement with a heavy heart.</u>

Our Song

I was dancing when the music stopped.
How dare you turn it off?
Now, I fumble with the radio dial,
Seeking our song in the static's trial.
November night, my pinnacle of bliss,
Attempting to resurrect what I miss –

I think it started with a swish, then a slow melody crept in,
And before we knew it – the snare drum hit, mingling with
my footsteps thudding against the grey concrete
to catch the last bus on Thursday eves.
The spring's songbirds harmonised with
the gulp of wine, a soft whisper of your words in my mind.
July rain and the spoon scraping tiramisu's plate
Faded into the chorus of your voice,
The first time you said you loved me.

Riddell Parade strolls, stormy evenings we zest.
Cinematic nights with popcorn in hand,
Embraces shared in cinema's glow,
Ben and Jerry's moments, spoons clinked slow.
Lorne's rocky shores, stove-tuned hum,
Monsoons and whispers, bedroom's soft strum.
The crinkling sound when your lips brushed my jacket
instead of cheeks of mine, somehow it felt just right.
Soft petals falling under strings' embrace,
A staccato of yells before we approached the bridge,
Oh how we resolved that fight, dreaming of lights
for our beautiful evenings inside.

Verses woven in the fabric of time's maze.
Recalled like notes in a nostalgic refrain.
October 05 returned, the drizzly musical set.
Empress of China, indulging in oily goodness,
Pizzas spanning Yarra Valley to queer Fitzroy's vastness.
Thinking of March 05, pure joy on my slate,
Yellow cardigan, once mine, found its fate,
Looked better on you, that January night's date.

I was dancing when the music stopped
Now, I must continue tuning the radio.

Taylor Swift – Happiness

A Conversation with Simran

No offence but, are you blind?
I mean, have you not savoured the allure of my smile?
How did you overlook my extraordinary essence,
a mystery that genuinely escapes my understanding?

Throughout our journey, did you not grasp the prowess of my mind –
to weave visions both sultry and refined?
I'm a tireless architect of ambition,
building towering peaks with unwavering might.
I'm driven, a relentless toiler emblazoning skies
with a shower of fireworks so bright!
Bejewelled with accolades, awards, and medals,
I bask in standing ovations,
crafting a legacy that leaves no room for reservations.

No, forget that, because I am the maestro of joy,
focusing on making others smile,
The proof was in your laughter each night!
I wield the spatula and broom with finesse,
crafting a haven of happiness.
I am adored, by my friends and family,
Bustling social life, a blast at parties!
I don't need the crutch of drugs nor
alcohol's hazy drive,
To get me fun and moving and
start conversations brilliant and bright!

A supportive shoulder, extended willingly in times of sorrow,
an attentive ear, expanding gladly
for rants, cries, and gossip to borrow.
In moments of doubt, shrouding my amazing essence,
friends, like nurturing parents, echo reassurances,
and when I feared the void of companionship,
Simran reassured, "Dude, your emotional availability is a treasure,
Only fools would forsake your charms,
a loss unmistakably theirs."

I mean, I have to agree, don't I?
I won't drag you down, but the loss is unmistakably yours.

Warm Orange.

No Right Time

There is no right time for the grief to kick in.
It is always an uninvited visitor.
Bringing a reason for people to come together, for shared
meals, for shared embraces, to show their true colours.
Appearing amidst the beautiful ballets, Kathak performances,
Grade 10 school plays and Vaisakhi Bhangra.
Diwali.

"Open the door, I am standing outside with your
friend"
Come in, enjoy the samosas. I've made chaat.
Do you want to wear the Kurtas, take polaroids on
this camera she got me for Christmas?
I've made him wear it, too. it looks good, doesn't
it?
The red one. It fits him well.
Stale samosas. Kitchen conversation. No place to
stand in the living room.
Marilyn stares down at the spilled coriander chutney
on the beige carpet.
"I'm going downstairs again, I need a breather"

Party, nay, a funeral.
White kurtas, some beige shirts,
A sea of white dupattas, in unison.
Sukhmani Sahib. Kirtan Sohila.
At 4 AM, he passed away,
and the mourning began—our elder's journey in a 6-hour passage,
tears flowing freely.
"You don't drink milk right after someone dies," another
unwritten rule of the ritual.
There's no right time for the grief to kick in.
Evening walks with a walking stick, a grandson declining to
accompany, and sleepy strolls.
April 9, Founder's day, marked the fall from which he never
rose, bedridden for a year.
The missing presence lingers, especially on the farm,
where visions of him visit my parents in the quietude of the
night.

No Right Time

One and a half months on the farm, contemplating life's
uncertainties and
the impending dismissal from the school play.
A mother absent from the audience,
green satin shirt seeking supporters.
"It is okay." The after-party unfolds –
a cake, some Pepsi, and chips –
an attempt at celebration overshadowed by the sting of
frugality.
Bloody misers!

I've kept the polaroids on my desk.
You're back! I know he is annoying you, but I hope you're
enjoying your day off, so far?
We're playing this Chinese game around the coffee table in the
living room,
"Your turn! Your turn!"
My turn! My turn!
Hushed requests – friends please stay,
it's not even 11PM!
The fun had only just begun.
That man is flirting with her sister,
"Oh, he is no good news"
"She's a grown woman now, but I'll let her know"
No sleep, I've graduated, let's just drink & enjoy.
The degree had kept me in a chokehold,
Maybe you could choke me?
And so you did...

Party, nay, a funeral.
White kurtas, some beige shirts,
A sea of white dupattas, in unison.
Sukhmani Sahib. Kirtan Sohila.
At 5AM, we got the call, she passed away.
The grandson kept away, barely able to touch her feet.
Lifeless grey woman in deep red.
Cloaked with pink dupattas.
She'll suffocate!
"You're young, you don't go to the cremation ground."
Regret lingers in the air. I didn't even see her face.
There's no right time for the grief to kick in.
Snakes and ladders – never materialised.
Summer vacations and warm embraces – never transpired.

No Right Time

Stories of life lived, life given, life shed — unshared.
Photo from the obituary kept under the folded clothes,
He still terrorises her.

Final examinations.
Rush! Go back home to prepare - don't waste your time there.
Hazy memories, multitude of hues.
Chemical formulas, that don't matter now.
but she still does - she always will.
suffocating, her legs didn't work,
"at least she got one of her sons married off before she
departed."
Sigh.
Play piano mid air -
'an ode to joy'
E-E-F-G-G-F-E-D-C-C-D-E-E-D-D, repeat.
The mother absent for a month, grieving her mother.
The father missing his wife, the kids missing their mother.
There is no right time for the grief to kick in.

"We have to dance to this song! It is my favourite bollywood
song!"
She is a little too drunk, don't mind us.
I am a little drunk, too. I giggle.
"I am wary of where he is going every couple of hours, smoking
perhaps?"
No he has told me he wants to go for breathers, every couple of
minutes,
He can't tolerate her boyfriend, and the other guy...
"You, me and her, lets take photos on her phone."
I know we're not related by blood, but we are like siblings,
for life.
I am very happy!
Are you?

Party, nay, it'll spread, the virus, funeral
Multi-coloured shirts, shorts and jeans
A smattering of colourful dupattas, in unison.
Sukhmani Sahib. Kirtan Sohila.
Middle of the day, I got the call, she passed away.
They've been on the farm for months now.
Trying to escape the daily deaths on the street.

No Right Time

Alas, burial—
"She made it this far, waiting for your birthday," forever
altering the celebration.
There is no right time for grief to kick in.
Dry nose replace the moist one,
a loyal companion now roams the farm.
For four years, we've planned a tree over her grave.
Perhaps this June, it'll manifest.

Cut cake, celebrate.
Rushed mourning, emotions brushed aside, a familiar routine.
Unable to visit her grave for two years,
Stranded on an island, distanced.
Much-needed hugs,
Conversations and reminiscing—hushed, confined to a 5-inch
screen.
A decade-old bond shattered, buried, cold,
Salt rubbed into wounds.
The departed vision, never to return,
Eyes clouded, bumping into sofas she once leaped upon,
Ears that once perked, now forever silent.
At least she's free from suffering.
Tears flowed the day before her passing; on the eleventh, I
couldn't cry.
Powerless to aid my sister, a brave face maintained.
There is no right time for the grief to kick in

The tequila bottle half-empty, the berry gin untouched.
Guests departing,
Mentally oscillating between A minor and E minor,
Strumming imaginary chords in the air.
Picking never came easy.
No! Stay!
"If he shows me another crystal DND Character, God Help me!"
alright, I'll talk to him; you relax.

No Right Time

                              Party, nay, a funeral
                      White kurtas, some beige shirts
                   A sea of white dupattas, in unison
                         Sukhmani Sahib. Kirtan Sohila.
                   The yellow bike I never got to ride
            At six o clock, he rode away without telling me.
                    What about his kids? His young wife?
                  What about her - A sister's plight?
    I regret not meeting him as much, I wish I had just called him
                                                          more
                                   What happened?
                                "Nobody knows."
         An infection, a parasite, the body's own cruel fuckery.
                There is no right time for the grief to kick in.
                I seldom spoke of him until that week in September,
                        and even then, not directly to him.
                   Unspoken words, unshared confessions,
               the weight of unspoken truths hangs in the air.

    How do you grieve someone who you don't have many memories
                                                           with?
                         I should be feeling more than I did
                  Locked in my room, trying to make the tears flow.
               Smell of sweet and sour pork outside is disgusting.
    Fuck! "You're not supposed to eat non-vegetarian food after the
                           death for a little while..."
                   There is no right time for the grief to kick in.
                       Thinking about my childhood —
         Growing up, I felt his gaze, yearning for a hug that never
                                               materialised.
         Fear, loneliness, and a terror that I could not understand
                                        then...*Him.*
            He's better now. His passing has made him slightly softer.
                                   At what cost?

"I think I'm hitting the bed."
"Downstairs for a walk, then."
Alright, we'll clean up in the morning.
Marilyn disapproves.

Paramjeet

I'm becoming a mirror
you capture your reflection in,
do you look distorted - do you still love your face?

does your tear roll back in,
holding up the mirror
knowing the mirror's me?

holding the mirror (me)
knowing the mirror's (you)

If it does, I know how much it took
how much of time you've given -
so you don't drop the mirror to the floor.

Your embrace is as warm as the autumn equinox -
as comfortable as the fields of cotton lace.
You hold me; I hold your gaze.

Jasleen

Come, let's plant a tree
in the garden, where its shade
touches your room, in the backyard,
with bright purple flowers.
We'll build a bay window so you can sit,
gazing out at lilac petals you painted
with your delicate hands.
I can't wait for you to show me.

Run towards me, twirl
in your pink dress. Revel
in your dance. You shine
brighter, reflecting light.

Sing in the car, no matter who listens or objects.
Take off that muzzle they've tried
to nail to your face.
Talk, scream,
let your thunderous zeal fill the air.

Speak with me, ask for help,
I'll say yes without need for convincing or bribe,
providing a shoulder -
always by your side.

Even when we see things in different hues,
know that I believe in you.
I know how your heart sinks
into your shoes,
and sometimes I wish I could wear them,
walk a while for you to breathe
a sigh of relief.

Experience every shade of life,
grow up with no tinge of regrets.
be independent, do not rely on any man,
I believe in you and

your spark and the ambition —
wear that coat, take that pencil,
write a beautiful narrative.
And while you do,
know you make me a better man.

Witness

Even if I can't do anything to—
save you, save them, save your children
I'll see—witness—
Your tragedy.

The oppression. The violence. The assault
on your rights, your bodies, your life—
Bound. Torn. Destroyed.
I will write and talk—
in languages they understand
and tell every passing person
about your struggles.

Anyone who reads—
will know of your freedom fight,
Injustice. Brutality. Courage.
The lashes on your
backs and on your smiles —
your husbands, your fathers, your sons' graceful eyes—
ripped apart sisters and daughters and mothers
set on fire.

I am seeing, witnessing—
Palestine, Kashmir, Congo, UP,
I am seeing, witnessing
the culpability of the leaders, white-skinned fiends, orange-
clad priests.
I am seeing, reading, absorbing -
the lynchings by vigilantes,
proclaimers of faiths, God's chosen men.

I am seeing —
my ancestors in your eyes, colour of my skin, the mouths of
delights—
I am melting at the sight—
the way sikhs were in '84.

I am witnessing —
People seize on lands unceded.
Rebellions. Living. Existence. Breathing. Rattling.
I am witnessing, and existing —
To pass on your stories
so you keep —
Rebelling. Living. Existing. Breathing.

Home 1.3

...and nobody cares if it is Monday, Thursday, or Saturday.
Friends keep meeting, dropping over at home, Food is fed,
and we don't have to plan it months in advance.
We drive past the Tuesday prayers outside the mandir
and hear the bells tolling away every couple of seconds.
We keep driving through the Corbusian veins and arteries,
driving over and over repetitively in circles,
again and again every two minutes or so,
unless you've dozed off waiting for the green light
at the Sector 22-35 roundabout.
...and nobody cares; we honk anyway.
It's not personal - we're just loud people.
We eat a lot, and we drive and eat and drive at the same time,
in a line from Sector 8 to Sector 10.
We love music so much that we play it aloud for everyone to
hear,
and we synchronise...and nobody cares.
We still find secret spots, undiscovered, quiet laneways
in the middle of the city.
It's not even a big city, but it surprises you when you find one
on a clandestine date in Sector 10 - the one you didn't enjoy,
but the gully was haunting, and it stuck to you like film photos
stick to one another.
I could swear it had been there since the 1800s.
And then there are some things you choose to ignore in this
city,
like the Green Citco bus drivers ignore the cars driving next
to them -
they just swerve
(because Chandigarh is a green city, and my car should be green
too).
Like people choose to ignore the same mela in Sector 34,
consistently on - all the time.
Yet I have never heard from anyone who's actually ever been
there,
unless once as a child being dragged by the parents, only once
though...
but the chaat in 34 is very lovely,
and I miss it, sitting away thousands of miles in a different
space...

How I (don't) want to die

Not a bullet's cold touch upon my head,
Nor betrayal's blade in the trust I've bred.

No explosive departure, a supernova's burst,
Or fragments of secrets in a concealed hearse.

Avoid the crash's grip or being shattered to dust,
Reduced to particles, a scattered bust.

I shun the flames that devour with cruel glee,
Or the icy grip that renders one's life free.

Frozen like icicles, dissolving into naught,
The sensation of tingling, a shared, eerie thought.

Forgotten or forgot, a chance unwilling to take
Hope I pass before I come to it.

I want to die, as peacefully as I came,
With people who love me beside my case.

Pitter, patter of raindrops on the window sill,
A fire crackling in the corner and friends laughing around me
still.

I want music I danced to in my 20s playing loud in the
background,
And flowers growing brightly on the vine outdoors.

Not a cosmic explosion, a fading star's cry,
But a caring presence till my last goodbye.

And if my story finishes before the final verse,
Grant me a semicolon, a connection to rehearse.

To find meaning in the unfinished narrative I leave,
A symbol of hope and continuation, I believe.

Yet, if closure eludes and destiny denies,
May love cradle my spirit as it gently flies.

Moving on

I trust my memories, not willingly, but relentlessly,
Unable to expel the residue of every kindness and cruelty.
No matter how hard I exhale, they cling like smoke to my lungs,
A hacking cough, days on end, a futile attempt to purge.
I give up trying.

Yet, a nagging fear creeps in,
I sense my memories eroding,
your eyes, your freckles, your lips, the shade of your hair.
The terracotta tee you wore cooking for me,
the red shirt and blue shorts on our first date,
the blue shirt and your granddad's leather jacket,
a frequent visitor to my place.
No more.

A conflict within, I yearn to move forward,
Make attempts, futile as they may be,
To not sit alone, consumed by thoughts of you,
Two and a half months now, counting the moments.
I'm haunted by the prospect—
what I once cherished will dwindle into oblivion,
a fading heartbeat rendered mute.
Lost in the passing of months, years,
Reduced to nothingness.

Yet, I grapple with the desire to clutch onto you,
to hoard the fragments of us,
fearing the loss of a self - intricately entwined with you.
I cradle this melancholy in my bones,
guarding it fiercely,
as the notion of forfeiting our shared history recoils,
much like you did when I first professed my love—
repeatedly, persistently, until you succumbed.

I find myself at odds with my mind, because I remember how
gradually my memories forgave and forgot,
my childhood best-friend and his betrayal,
but his didn't sink its teeth in my body like you did,

I grapple with my thoughts, as people morph into wistful whispers,
Like the playmate from the park at age five, now a fleeting dream.
However, his departure wasn't marked by duplicity, life just unfolded.

Then I think of the friend whose life I glimpse on the internet,
reminiscing every Sunday afternoon at his place, with him, his sister, and mine,
the quartet that played the best beats, I can't even recall how he exited my life but he did.
Observing him and his sister, I don't fully grasp where it went wrong, but life just decided to sweep them away.

At odds with my brain, found it easy to hate and detach
from a friend on whose birthday it would pour each year,
fighting storms to be by his side, now not even thinking about his life.
However, his hurting me came from loyalty to someone else, accepted it as life's growing trends.

A struggle persists within my head,
Choosing self-respect and happiness over connection,
The ten-year friend fades, yet her disrespect pales,
Unable to brown my goldfinch yellows that you once owned.

Maybe back then, I was wounded, and their betrayals did sting and burn like yours did,
Maybe I was shaken to my core after their departure, as well,
Maybe I did want to hold on to their lives in mine as much as I do yours,
and that's why I'm wary of my brain and the tricks it might play
to aid me in moving on and eventually forgetting you, despite my unwillingness.

Until We Let Them Go...

I saw her, brimming with vigour and glee,
Living life on her own terms, wild and free.
Venturing to places beyond my dreams' expanse,
Embracing life as if it were crafted for her to dance.

I didn't know her well, just glimpses here and there,
Only her name, unsure if she knew mine to share.
Whispers of her beauty filled the air,
Or was it 'her beauty fills,' to be fair?

Her cheeks blushed red, shimmering gold in the light,
As she sang, bidding another day goodbye.
A budding artist, painting her future bright,
Against the Stygian night, a mesmerising sight.

Dark, mysterious, and enigmatic her mind,
Uncertain if destiny would be kind.
Why did she doubt herself, I ponder,
Such thoughts, unjust, causing her to wander.

And then after months, or maybe years, I don't remember.
She flew away, like sand off the desert.
Travelling away miles and miles, I felt her beside my ears.
"She is gone !" Someone said to me.

She lingers, her spirit undeniably connected,
Her essence endures, forever protected.
People won't depart unless we let them fly,
In our hearts and minds, their memories lie.

She is here, I know she is.
She is not gone until we let her go.
She is connected, I know it so.
People don't fly until we let them go.

Home 2.1

How pretty are those purple pink skies,
they are out of this world, yet here we are,
Clinking our whites to these beautiful summer nights!

They are rare, and so are you,
When I first met you, I hated your guts, my mate,
so temperamental, I see your phases change within seconds.

In your corduroy op-shop jacket,
Did you really think you'd solve world's problems sipping on
your lukewarm, oat-milk latte from your Frank Green flask?

You know how much I love you now,
took a while to accept your cold sting, it feels like warmth
now –
a comforting clutch which helps me shed my mask.

How you've grown on me, a mystery deep,
I guess those are the friendships that stand the test of times,
there was no need to force this friendship, so I felt freedom
to be myself.

There are moments where I feel I'll have to leave you behind,
for a calling that's my duty, one I can't deny.
I have seen many break their promises, but I am not of the
kind, you know.

Perhaps, I'll keep myself anchored somewhere in the middle,
come over, stay for the weekend at your house,
and eat delicious pies at your dinner table, like we are doing
right now.

Maybe that evening, the sky won't be as vibrant pink,
maybe a shade of orange or blue that we would have never seen,
but I promise we'll be clinking our glasses that day too.
Perhaps, a Red would better suit?

Myrtle, Daisy & Lavender

So much love and kindness resides in her,
Incredibly and immaculately, she weaves for me a bouquet of -
Myrtle, Daisy and Lavender.
Ribbon knotted into a bow around the stems so tender,
A sweet fragrance of her mind and effort seeps through air
That I can't help but bask in.

Soulmates

Perched side by side, atop the wall so high,
Happily laughing about the world's wonders and sighs
with twinkling little stars in our eyes.
Abruptly, the King's men, with cruel might,
Shoved us down, leaving us to plummet and find.
Two eggs cracked, like shattered hopes, in the fall,
We clung to each other
enduring heartache unlike any other before;
we granted each other space to feel our truths,
Allowing ourselves to fracture, letting insides flow.
Your staunchest ally, an unwavering cheer in the storm,
"I love your brain!" she declares so happily,
Consistent as sunrise, it happens every time.
She calls me at 2AM, dead asleep - mobile on DnD,
Sorry! - Good Morning texts
asking - "How are we today?"
a five-hour-long phone conversation
in the middle of the day.
Ice cream on the park bench, swinging on kids' swingset –
Golden hour, seagulls sing on the blonde sand.
Dancing in the kitchen, tipsy on cheap wine,
laughter in the air, midnight coast-line drives,
In each other's arms, we thrive –
holding each other in tears, lending a shoulder to lean,
Celebrating our little wins, moments unseen –
After crying and waiting for the king's horses and the men to
show,
We decided to eventually put ourselves back together with gold.
Under the diamonds in the skies so dark,
We began plastering each other's cracks with a potion full of
heart –
a mixture of teardrops, cardamom, shortbread so sweet,
stirred together with yummy milk tea.

Romanticisation

I've loved the idea of pretty lights, small apartments,
bronze hues on true blues,
where swans go for rides.
I've loved the idea of a tranquil garden with picturesque
landscapes,
Tudor homes, tiled roofs and cobblestone walkways.
Wrought iron decorative jails, dust kissed carpets.
English oak, Ash trees and Hawthorn leaves.
Red boxes, stone structures, medieval relics.
Even lamb shepherds upon grass covered rocky hills.
I've adored the notion of a language binding all places I've
been and will go.
Even romanticised the grey skies, incessant rains, and
isolating chills.

Yet, it's all still cold, biting;
Never fulfilling, ever elusive,
Faded, sagey, dull and gloomy.
I want to dive, but it doesn't let me.
Uninviting, shallower than the Pond in my *Pind*.
Just like *him*.

I want warm embrace of Gajarela.
I want to fall back in love with my golden fields,
sprawling lawns, the sunny dreams.
Turquoise Blue Canals, tube-well water in the childhood summer
heat.
I want to fall back in love with my home where my stomach never
rumbles,
The rock garden, red sandstone marvels, intricate marble
jaalis,
Pipal, Neem, Shisham, Kikkar.
The expansive enveloping of snow-capped mountains,
The arid deserts and bustling bazaars bursting
with intertwined colours, scents, and sheen.
The scripts of gurus, the melodies from my mother's womb,
the *kirtan*, the *baanis*.

I want to romanticise myself and what's truly mine.

I have not seen enough

Believe me, I understand the vastness of our world.
I yearn for more — the unseen, the untold,
For all my senses to be awakened, and new stories to behold.
My heart begs to stray — to be far, far away!

I want to go to Japan, see the cherry blossoms bloom,
Listen to the Italian Cheese & Wine whispering tales old and
new.
These rose-gold Parisian skies entice a kiss so divine.
I know, like a dog, I'll exclaim at my reflection in Bolivia,
where skies and land truly blend.

Shiver, gazing at the Northern lights dancing in hues of green
and pink!
Wear happy yellow raincoats under the grey showers in Reading.
Share a meal with Egyptian Queens adorned in headscarves of
splendour.
Oh, please take me to Gabon's jungles, I want to breathe!

To Chicago to see Sulllivan's marvels in the icy breeze!
and meet the Gods under Athens' Ninth Heavens, so to speak.
If I feel lost, I am sure deep in Kenyan Savannah, I'll find my
way,
Will be sure to come up with new ideas floating in the Dead Sea.

Women in Spain, captivating and mystique.
and in lands where allure resides in men, igniting a passion so
fierce.
Their captivating tales and the stories to share,
I'll immerse myself, willingly, I dare.

Experiencing the Dutch high with no care,
Through Lahore's gateways, I'll traverse the history laid bare,
In Afghan's Mughal Gardens, resilient tales unfold.
Please take me away, I have not seen enough!

There is so much in the world that I am eager for.
Experiences and love, and to have my stories told.
After the wonders and adventures I have properly seen —
I want to come home and peacefully sleep.

26

In this topsy-turvy world of excesses and absences,
You're neither too much nor too little, it seems
for the right ones, you're grand!
Keep that child-like wonder, like holding orchids in your hand.

The cape of kindness looks good on you, wear it with grace,
If ever, you find yourself unkind, in humanity find a trace.
You're a brilliant kaleidoscope, let your colours shine in your
splendid array,
Multitudes within, let them see the light of day.

Your parents want your best, though you know the way,
Your best is defined by you, you have the final say.
You'll be angry and it'll feel like a teenage summer storm;
It too will pass, revealing a peaceful inner form.

Diversity is life's grand gift and design,
Like it or not, nobody shares the same heart's line
Nor do they share the taste, sound, and the world's view,
They're as varied as the skies in spring, different and true.

Please give it your all, don't doubt your might,
In the journey, see who's with you along for the ride.
No true black or white, just greys in between,
Trust your intuition, let your faith be seen.

Love as you do, without floodgates, let it flow,
Explain, educate, don't rush to judge. Be slow.
Grow into yourself, it is a celebration rare,
Even if you're alone, let self-love be your flare.

You'll face challenges, be proud of the effort put in,
Appreciate the process, not just the win.
Life can be harsh, despite its poetic touch,
Listen. No one deserves an unkind, mental march.

Chances granted, but a shoe-horn don't be,
Stand firm, let your spirit roam free.
Open your hearts, listen with ears attuned with care,
Yet if silence lingers, don't bother, don't despair.

Respect your beliefs and theirs, let them evolve,
But don't let them be chains, let them dissolve.
Sometimes, go where the road takes you.
Other times, stand up, speak out, let your voice grow.

Unlearn self-hate, the standards are far too high,
Love yourself as you love the flawed autumn sky.
Your mind is a wily stupid friend
pause, reflect, let the wisdom end.

Celebrate the life, man, it's your garden party's bloom,
For the sunflowers with you, dispel any gloom.

Curtain Fall

Ladies, gentlemen & my non binary pals,
I hope you've enjoyed the show.
Review it, give it stars, or not,
or wait until I finish this monologue to -

Throw tomatoes, shoes, or flowers if you may,
I'll receive any token showing you stayed
until the very end, on my journey through
all that I've prepared just for you.

Perhaps we'll meet again, who can say?
I'll see you then with more stories to relay.
Of love, heartbreaks, betrayals, and fest,
More firsts, more lasts, more of life's best.

And if I made you uncomfortable, I'm sorry,
I apologise to all for any worry.
Especially if you saw yourself in my tales,
I'm sorry, I'm glad, whichever prevails.

I promise I've tried to keep you concealed,
But hope my stories helped and healed.

Before you depart, take a moment to reflect,
Collect your tokens, show your respect.
Hold your loved ones close, form a single file,
As I bow and the curtain falls, exit with a smile.

Thank you.

26th | Epilogue

On my 26th birthday, I made some chocolate waffles in a waffle maker, a present from one of my closest friends. The evening before, friends masterminded a party for me which enveloped me in a cosy fug. Their love wrapped around me like a warm blanket, soothing parts of my soul that were hurting. At Midnight, my phone was inundated by calls from family and friends. From near and far. It painted my night with bright colours of love that momentarily eclipsed any sense of loneliness. Amidst beautiful gifts, cards, and messages, I wondered about my tendency to lament love's absence. My obnoxious obliviousness to the abundant warmth that surrounds me sickens me.

As I savoured each bite of those waffles, I couldn't help but reflect on the unwavering love and forgiveness. Despite my flaws and imperfections, there is a profound sense of gratitude for the unconditional love that embraces me. Though my insecurities often whisper doubts about my worthiness of such love, my heart soars with the realisation of how blessed I am to have it in abundance.

As I meticulously combed through this anthology of my thoughts and experiences, editing and selecting each poem within this collection, I am struck by the journey of my life that has led me here. Beyond the tumultuous emotions of youth, beyond the trials of love and loss. This collection was born from a wish to understand myself, becoming a mirror reflecting back the essence of who I am and why I am that way. In doing so, it has captured the pain, the love, the confusion, and the growth that defines me.

So here it is, dear reader, a glimpse into 26 years of experiences and thoughts. I hope you find pieces that resonate with you, inviting moments of reflection and sparking introspection. May you return, just as I will, to revisit these pages and relive 26 years of memories.

Oh, and the waffles, too, were delightful!

The Poet

Mannik Singh, 26, is an Indian writer. Mannik was born in Ferozepur, Punjab and lived in Chandigarh until the age of 19. He studied at the Yadavindra Public School before moving to Melbourne, Australia to pursue his tertiary education in Architecture at the University of Melbourne.

As of 2024, he works as an Architectural Graduate in Melbourne.

Mannik started writing poetry in high-school when he was trying to escape into the secret wardrobes, or wondrous worlds within his mind, weave stories of his fantasies and caprices. Inspired by the timeless verse of Emily Dickinson, particularly her poignant reflection on mortality in "Because I could not stop for Death," Mannik embarked on a journey of self-discovery through poetry.

His current influences include Emily Dickinson, Taylor Swift, Chen Chen, Marge Piercy, Sam Sax, Ocean Vuong, Halsey, Aga Shahid Ali & Akhil Katyal.

To read/view more of the Mannik's works and get regular updates

www.manniksingh.com
www.instagram.com/mannik_singh